Just The

Textbook Key Facts

Textbook Outlines, Highlights, and Practice Quizzes

BSCS Biology: A Molecular Approach

by McGraw-Hill Glencoe, 9th Edition

All "Just the Facts101" Material Written or Prepared by Cram101 Textbook Reviews

Title Page

STUDYING MADE EASY

This FactsI0I notebook is designed to make studying easier and increase your comprehension of the textbook material. Instead of starting with a blank notebook and trying to write down everything discussed in class lectures, you can use this FactsI0I textbook notebook and annotate your notes along with the lecture.

Our goal is to give you the best tools for success.

For a supreme understanding of the course, pair your notebook with our online tools. Should you decide you prefer jtfl0l.com as your study tool,

we'd like to offer you a trade...

Our Trade In program is a simple way for us to keep our promise and provide you the best studying tools, regardless of where you purchased your FactsI0I textbook notebook. As long as your notebook is in *Like New Condition**, you can send it back to us and we will immediately give you a JustTheFactsI0I.com account free for 120 days!

Let The *Trade In* Begin!

THREE SIMPLE STEPS TO TRADE:

1. Go to www.jtf101.com/tradein and fill out the packing slip information.

2. Submit and print the packing slip and mail it in with your FactsI0I textbook notebook.

3. Activate your account after you receive your email confirmation.

* Books must be returned in *Like New Condition*, meaning there is no damage to the book including, but not limited to; ripped or torn pages, markings or writing on pages, or folded / creased pages. Upon receiving the book, FactsI0I will inspect it and reserves the right to terminate your free FactsI0I.com account and return your textbook notebook at the owners expense.

LEARNING SYSTEM

"Just the Facts101" is a Content Technologies publication and tool designed to give you all the facts from your textbook. Visit JustTheFacts101.com for the full practice test for each of your chapters for virtually any of your textbooks.

Facts101 has built custom study tools specific to your textbook. We provide all of the factual testable information and unlike traditional study guides, we will never send you back to your textbook for more information.

YOU WILL NEVER HAVE TO HIGHLIGHT A BOOK AGAIN!

Facts101 StudyGuides

All of the information in this StudyGuide is written specifically for your textbook. We include the key terms, places, people, and concepts... the information you can expect on your next exam!

Want to take a practice test?

Throughout each chapter of this StudyGuide you will find links to JustTheFacts101.com where you can select specific chapters to take a complete test on, or you can subscribe and get practice tests for up to 12 of your textbooks, along with other exclusive Jtf101.com tools like problem solving labs and reference libraries.

JustTheFacts101.com

Only Jtf101.com gives you the outlines, highlights, and PRACTICE TESTS specific to your textbook. JustTheFacts101.com is an online application where you'll discover study tools designed to make the most of your limited study time.

By purchasing this book, you get 50% off the normal monthly subscription fee!. Just enter the promotional code **'DK73DW24123'** on the Jtf101.com registration screen.

www.JustTheFacts101.com

BSCS Biology: A Molecular Approach
McGraw-Hill Glencoe, 9th

CONTENTS

1. The Chemistry of Life

CHAPTER OUTLINE: KEY TERMS, PEOPLE, PLACES, CONCEPTS

Biofilm

Hydra

Intron

Growth hormone

Antibody

Carbohydrate

Disaccharide

Glucose

Monosaccharide

Polysaccharide

Cellulose

Glycogen

Lactose

Maltose

Sucrose

Triglyceride

Unsaturated fat

Lipid

Cholesterol

Phospholipid

Protein

1. The Chemistry of Life

	Saturated fat
	Amino acid
	Peptide
	Deoxyribose
	Nucleic acid
	Nucleotide
	Ribose
	Double Helix
	Genetic code

CHAPTER HIGHLIGHTS & NOTES: KEY TERMS, PEOPLE, PLACES, CONCEPTS

Biofilm	A biofilm is any group of microorganisms in which cells stick to each other on a surface. These adherent cells are frequently embedded within a self-produced matrix of extracellular polymeric substance (EPS). Biofilm EPS, which is also referred to as slime (although not everything described as slime is a biofilm), is a polymeric conglomeration generally composed of extracellular DNA, proteins, and polysaccharides.
Hydra	Hydra is a genus of small, simple, fresh-water animals that possess radial symmetry. Hydra are predatory animals belonging to the phylum Cnidaria and the class Hydrozoa. They can be found in most unpolluted fresh-water ponds, lakes, and streams in the temperate and tropical regions and can be found by gently sweeping a collecting net through weedy areas.
Intron	An intron is any nucleotide sequence within a gene that is removed by RNA splicing while the final mature RNA product of a gene is being generated. The term intron refers to both the DNA sequence within a gene and the corresponding sequence in RNA transcripts. Sequences that are joined together in the final mature RNA after RNA splicing are exons.

Growth hormone	Growth hormone, also known as somatotropin or somatropin, is a peptide hormone that stimulates growth, cell reproduction and regeneration in humans and other animals. It is a type of mitogen which is specific only to certain kinds of cells. Growth hormone is a 191-amino acid, single-chain polypeptide that is synthesized, stored, and secreted by somatotropic cells within the lateral wings of the anterior pituitary gland.
Antibody	An antibody, also known as an immunoglobulin (Ig), is a large Y-shaped protein produced by B cells that is used by the immune system to identify and neutralize foreign objects such as bacteria and viruses. The antibody recognizes a unique part of the foreign target, called an antigen. Each tip of the 'Y' of an antibody contains a paratope (a structure analogous to a lock) that is specific for one particular epitope (similarly analogous to a key) on an antigen, allowing these two structures to bind together with precision.
Carbohydrate	A carbohydrate is an organic compound comprising only carbon, hydrogen, and oxygen, usually with a hydrogen:oxygen atom ratio of 2:1 ; in other words, with the empirical formula $C_m(H_2O)_n$ (where m could be different from n). Some exceptions exist; for example, deoxyribose, a sugar component of DNA, has the empirical formula $C_5H_{10}O_4$. Carbohydrates are technically hydrates of carbon; structurally it is more accurate to view them as polyhydroxy aldehydes and ketones.
Disaccharide	A disaccharide or biose is the carbohydrate formed when two monosaccharides undergo a condensation reaction which involves the elimination of a small molecule, such as water, from the functional groups only. Like monosaccharides, disaccharides form an aqueous solution when dissolved in water. Three common examples are sucrose, lactose, and maltose.
Glucose	Glucose, meaning 'sweet'. The suffix '-ose' denotes a sugar.
Monosaccharide	Monosaccharides are the most basic units of carbohydrates. They are the simplest form of sugar and are usually colorless, water-soluble, crystalline solids. Some monosaccharides have a sweet taste.
Polysaccharide	Polysaccharides are long carbohydrate molecules of monosaccharide units joined together by glycosidic bonds. They range in structure from linear to highly branched. Polysaccharides are often quite heterogeneous, containing slight modifications of the repeating unit.
Cellulose	Cellulose is an organic compound with the formula n, a polysaccharide consisting of a linear chain of several hundred to over ten thousand ß(1?4) linked -glucose units. Cellulose is an important structural component of the primary cell wall of green plants, many forms of algae and the oomycetes. Some species of bacteria secrete it to form biofilms.
Glycogen	Glycogen is a multibranched polysaccharide of glucose that serves as a form of energy storage in animals and fungi. The polysaccharide structure represents the main storage form of glucose in the body.

1. The Chemistry of Life

Lactose	Lactose is a disaccharide sugar derived from galactose and glucose that is found in milk. Lactose makes up around 0-8% of milk (by weight), although the amount varies among species and individuals. It is extracted from sweet or sour whey.
Maltose	Maltose, also known as maltobiose or malt sugar, is a disaccharide formed from two units of glucose joined with an a(1?4) bond, formed from a condensation reaction. The isomer isomaltose has two glucose molecules linked through an a(1?6) bond. Maltose is the second member of an important biochemical series of glucose chains.
Sucrose	Sucrose is the organic compound commonly known as table sugar and sometimes called saccharose. A white, odorless, crystalline powder with a sweet taste, it is best known for its role in food. The molecule is a disaccharide composed of the monosaccharides glucose and fructose with the molecular formula $C_{12}H_{22}O_{11}$.
Triglyceride	Low-density lipoprotein is one of the five major groups of lipoproteins, which, in order of molecular size, largest to smallest, are chylomicrons, very low-density lipoprotein (VLDL), intermediate-density lipoprotein (IDL), LDL, and high-density lipoprotein (HDL). Lipoprotein molecules enable the transportation of lipids (fats), such as cholesterol, phospholipids, and triglycerides, within the water around cells (extracellular fluid), including the bloodstream. Studies have shown that higher levels of type-B LDL particles (as opposed to type-A LDL particles) are associated with health problems, including cardiovascular disease.
Unsaturated fat	An unsaturated fat is a fat or fatty acid in which there is at least one double bond within the fatty acid chain. A fatty acid chain is monounsaturated if it contains one double bond, and polyunsaturated if it contains more than one double bond. Where double bonds are formed, hydrogen atoms are eliminated.
Lipid	Lipids are a group of naturally occurring molecules that include fats, waxes, sterols, fat-soluble vitamins, monoglycerides, diglycerides, triglycerides, phospholipids, and others. The main biological functions of lipids include storing energy, signaling, and acting as structural components of cell membranes. Lipids have applications in the cosmetic and food industries as well as in nanotechnology.
Cholesterol	Cholesterol, from the Ancient Greek chole- and stereos (solid) followed by the chemical suffix -ol for an alcohol, is an organic molecule. It is a sterol (or modified steroid), and an essential structural component of animal cell membranes that is required to establish proper membrane permeability and fluidity. Cholesterol is thus considered within the class of lipid molecules.
Phospholipid	Phospholipids are a class of lipids that are a major component of all cell membranes as they can form lipid bilayers. Most phospholipids contain a diglyceride, a phosphate group, and a simple organic molecule such as choline; one exception to this rule is sphingomyelin, which is derived from sphingosine instead of glycerol.

The first phospholipid identified as such in biological tissues was lecithin, or phosphatidylcholine, in the egg yolk, by Theodore Nicolas Gobley, a French chemist and pharmacist, in 1847. The structure of the phospholipid molecule generally consists of hydrophobic tails and a hydrophilic head.

Protein	Proteins are large biological molecules, or macromolecules, consisting of one or more chains of amino acids. Proteins perform a vast array of functions within living organisms, including catalyzing metabolic reactions, replicating DNA, responding to stimuli, and transporting molecules from one location to another. Proteins differ from one another primarily in their sequence of amino acids, which is dictated by the nucleotide sequence of their genes, and which usually results in folding of the protein into a specific three-dimensional structure that determines its activity.
Saturated fat	Saturated fat is fat that consists of triglycerides containing only saturated fatty acids. Saturated fatty acids have no double bonds between the individual carbon atoms of the fatty acid chain. That is, the chain of carbon atoms is fully 'saturated' with hydrogen atoms.
Amino acid	Amino acids are biologically important organic compounds made from amine ($-NH_2$) and carboxylic acid ($-COOH$) functional groups, along with a side-chain specific to each amino acid. The key elements of an amino acid are carbon, hydrogen, oxygen, and nitrogen, though other elements are found in the side-chains of certain amino acids. About 500 amino acids are known and can be classified in many ways.
Peptide	Peptides are short chains of amino acid monomers linked by peptide bonds. The covalent chemical bonds are formed when the carboxyl group of one amino acid reacts with the amino group of another. The shortest peptides are dipeptides, consisting of 2 amino acids joined by a single peptide bond, followed by tripeptides, tetrapeptides, etc.
Deoxyribose	Deoxyribose, or more precisely 2-deoxyribose, is a monosaccharide with idealized formula H--(CH_2)-$(CHOH)_3$-H. Its name indicates that it is a deoxy sugar, meaning that it is derived from the sugar ribose by loss of an oxygen atom. Since the pentose sugars arabinose and ribose only differ by the stereochemistry at C2', 2-deoxyribose and 2-deoxyarabinose are equivalent, although the latter term is rarely used because ribose, not arabinose, is the precursor to deoxyribose.
Nucleic acid	Nucleic acids are polymeric macromolecules, or large biological molecules, essential for all known forms of life. Nucleic acids, which include DNA (deoxyribonucleic acid) and RNA (ribonucleic acid), are made from monomers known as nucleotides. Each nucleotide has three components: a 5-carbon sugar, a phosphate group, and a nitrogenous base.
Nucleotide	Nucleotides are organic molecules that serve as the monomers, or subunits, of nucleic acids like DNA and RNA. The building blocks of nucleic acids, nucleotides are composed of a nitrogenous base, a five-carbon sugar (ribose or deoxyribose), and at least one phosphate group.

1. The Chemistry of Life

	Nucleotides serve to carry packets of energy within the cell (ATP). In the form of the nucleoside triphosphates (ATP, GTP, CTP and UTP), nucleotides play central roles in metabolism.
Ribose	Ribose is an organic compound with the formula $C_5H_{10}O_5$; specifically, a monosaccharide with linear form $H-(C=O)-(CHOH)_4-H$, which has all the hydroxyl groups on the same side in the Fischer projection. The term may refer to either of two enantiomers. The term usually indicates -ribose, which occurs widely in nature and is discussed here.
Double Helix	Double Helix, a novel by Nancy Werlin, is about 18-year old Eli Samuels, who works for a famous molecular biologist named Dr. Quincy Wyatt. There is a mysterious connection between Dr. Wyatt and Eli's parents, and all Eli knows about the connection is that it has something to do with his mother, who has Huntington's disease. Because of the connection between Dr. Wyatt and the Samuels family, Eli's father is strongly against Eli working there.
Genetic code	The genetic code is the set of rules by which information encoded within genetic material is translated into proteins by living cells. Biological decoding is accomplished by the ribosome, which links amino acids in an order specified by mRNA, using transfer RNA (tRNA) molecules to carry amino acids and to read the mRNA three nucleotides at a time. The genetic code is highly similar among all organisms and can be expressed in a simple table with 64 entries.

1. _____s are large biological molecules, or macromolecules, consisting of one or more chains of amino acids. _____s perform a vast array of functions within living organisms, including catalyzing metabolic reactions, replicating DNA, responding to stimuli, and transporting molecules from one location to another. _____s differ from one another primarily in their sequence of amino acids, which is dictated by the nucleotide sequence of their genes, and which usually results in folding of the _____ into a specific three-dimensional structure that determines its activity.

    a. Protein
    b. BISC
    c. CASTp
    d. Deproteination

2. . A _____ is any group of microorganisms in which cells stick to each other on a surface. These adherent cells are frequently embedded within a self-produced matrix of extracellular polymeric substance (EPS).

_____ EPS, which is also referred to as slime (although not everything described as slime is a _____), is a polymeric conglomeration generally composed of extracellular DNA, proteins, and polysaccharides.

a. Bacterial outer membrane
b. Biological membrane
c. Biofilm
d. N-Acetylglucosamine

3. _____ is a genus of small, simple, fresh-water animals that possess radial symmetry. _____ are predatory animals belonging to the phylum Cnidaria and the class Hydrozoa. They can be found in most unpolluted fresh-water ponds, lakes, and streams in the temperate and tropical regions and can be found by gently sweeping a collecting net through weedy areas.

a. Barley
b. Hydra
c. Bombyx mori
d. Botryllus schlosseri

4. An _____, also known as an immunoglobulin (Ig), is a large Y-shaped protein produced by B cells that is used by the immune system to identify and neutralize foreign objects such as bacteria and viruses. The _____ recognizes a unique part of the foreign target, called an antigen. Each tip of the 'Y' of an _____ contains a paratope (a structure analogous to a lock) that is specific for one particular epitope (similarly analogous to a key) on an antigen, allowing these two structures to bind together with precision.

a. 3-Hydroxyaspartic acid
b. Antibody
c. Glycoalkaloid
d. Solamargine

5. _____, also known as somatotropin or somatropin, is a peptide hormone that stimulates growth, cell reproduction and regeneration in humans and other animals. It is a type of mitogen which is specific only to certain kinds of cells. _____ is a 191-amino acid, single-chain polypeptide that is synthesized, stored, and secreted by somatotropic cells within the lateral wings of the anterior pituitary gland.

a. Betatrophin
b. Big gastrin
c. Growth hormone
d. Bradykinin

---

1. a
2. c
3. b
4. b
5. c

You can take the complete Chapter Practice Test

for 1. The Chemistry of Life
on all key terms, persons, places, and concepts.

Online 99 Cents

http://www.JustTheFacts101.com

Use www.JustTheFacts101.com for all your study needs

including Facts101's online interactive problem solving labs in

chemistry, statistics, mathematics, and more.

2. Energy, Life, and the Biosphere

CHAPTER OUTLINE: KEY TERMS, PEOPLE, PLACES, CONCEPTS

Nutrient

Active site

Enzyme

Antibody

Radical

Glycogen

Intracellular

Amylase

Intron

Maltose

Carbohydrate

DNA replication

Gastrin

Protein

Bile

Lipase

Pepsin

Secretin

Trypsin

Biofilm

Nutrient	A nutrient is a chemical that an organism needs to live and grow or a substance used in an organism's metabolism which must be taken in from its environment. They are used to build and repair tissues, regulate body processes and are converted to and used as energy. Methods for nutrient intake vary, with animals and protists consuming foods that are digested by an internal digestive system, but most plants ingest nutrients directly from the soil through their roots or from the atmosphere.
Active site	In biology, the active site is the small portion of an enzyme where substrate molecules bind and undergo a chemical reaction. This chemical reaction occurs when a substrate collides with and slots into the active site of an enzyme. The active site is usually found in a 3-D groove or pocket of the enzyme, lined with amino acid residues (or nucleotides in RNA enzymes).
Enzyme	Enzymes are large biological molecules responsible for the thousands of metabolic processes that sustain life. They are highly selective catalysts, greatly accelerating both the rate and specificity of metabolic reactions, from the digestion of food to the synthesis of DNA. Most enzymes are proteins, although some catalytic RNA molecules have been identified. Enzymes adopt a specific three-dimensional structure, and may employ organic (e.g. biotin) and inorganic (e.g. magnesium ion) cofactors to assist in catalysis.
Antibody	An antibody, also known as an immunoglobulin (Ig), is a large Y-shaped protein produced by B cells that is used by the immune system to identify and neutralize foreign objects such as bacteria and viruses. The antibody recognizes a unique part of the foreign target, called an antigen. Each tip of the 'Y' of an antibody contains a paratope (a structure analogous to a lock) that is specific for one particular epitope (similarly analogous to a key) on an antigen, allowing these two structures to bind together with precision.
Radical	In chemistry, a radical is an atom, molecule, or ion that has unpaired valence electrons or an open electron shell, and therefore may be seen as having one or more 'dangling' covalent bonds.
	With some exceptions, these 'dangling' bonds make free radicals highly chemically reactive towards other substances, or even towards themselves: their molecules will often spontaneously dimerize or polymerize if they come in contact with each other. Most radicals are reasonably stable only at very low concentrations in inert media or in vacuum.
Glycogen	Glycogen is a multibranched polysaccharide of glucose that serves as a form of energy storage in animals and fungi. The polysaccharide structure represents the main storage form of glucose in the body.
	In humans, glycogen is made and stored primarily in the cells of the liver and the muscles, and functions as the secondary long-term energy storage (with the primary energy stores being fats held in adipose tissue).

2. Energy, Life, and the Biosphere

Intracellular	In cell biology, molecular biology and related fields, the word intracellular means 'inside the cell'. It is used in contrast to extracellular . The cell membrane (and, in many organisms, the cell wall) is the barrier between the two, and chemical composition of intra- and extracellular milieu can be radically different.
Amylase	Amylase is an enzyme that catalyses the hydrolysis of starch into sugars. Amylase is present in the saliva of humans and some other mammals, where it begins the chemical process of digestion. Foods that contain much starch but little sugar, such as rice and potato, taste slightly sweet as they are chewed because amylase turns some of their starch into sugar in the mouth.
Intron	An intron is any nucleotide sequence within a gene that is removed by RNA splicing while the final mature RNA product of a gene is being generated. The term intron refers to both the DNA sequence within a gene and the corresponding sequence in RNA transcripts. Sequences that are joined together in the final mature RNA after RNA splicing are exons.
Maltose	Maltose, also known as maltobiose or malt sugar, is a disaccharide formed from two units of glucose joined with an a(1?4) bond, formed from a condensation reaction. The isomer isomaltose has two glucose molecules linked through an a(1?6) bond. Maltose is the second member of an important biochemical series of glucose chains.
Carbohydrate	A carbohydrate is an organic compound comprising only carbon, hydrogen, and oxygen, usually with a hydrogen:oxygen atom ratio of 2:1 ; in other words, with the empirical formula $C_m(H_2O)_n$ (where m could be different from n). Some exceptions exist; for example, deoxyribose, a sugar component of DNA, has the empirical formula $C_5H_{10}O_4$. Carbohydrates are technically hydrates of carbon; structurally it is more accurate to view them as polyhydroxy aldehydes and ketones.
DNA replication	DNA replication is the process of producing two identical copies from one original DNA molecule. This biological process occurs in all living organisms and is the basis for biological inheritance. DNA is composed of two strands and each strand of the original DNA molecule serves as template for the production of the complementary strand, a process referred to as semiconservative replication.
Gastrin	In humans, gastrin is a peptide hormone that stimulates secretion of gastric acid by the parietal cells of the stomach and aids in gastric motility. It is released by G cells in the antrum of the stomach (the portion of the stomach adjacent the pyloric valve), duodenum, and the pancreas. Gastrin binds to cholecystokinin B receptors to stimulate the release of histamines in enterochromaffin-like cells, and it induces the insertion of K^+/H^+ ATPase pumps into the apical membrane of parietal cells (which in turn increases H^+ release into the stomach cavity).

Protein	Proteins are large biological molecules, or macromolecules, consisting of one or more chains of amino acids. Proteins perform a vast array of functions within living organisms, including catalyzing metabolic reactions, replicating DNA, responding to stimuli, and transporting molecules from one location to another. Proteins differ from one another primarily in their sequence of amino acids, which is dictated by the nucleotide sequence of their genes, and which usually results in folding of the protein into a specific three-dimensional structure that determines its activity.
Bile	Bile or gall is a bitter-tasting, dark green to yellowish brown fluid, produced by the liver of most vertebrates, that aids the digestion of lipids in the small intestine. In many species, bile is stored in the gallbladder and, when the organism eats, is discharged into the duodenum. Bile is 85% water, 10% bile salts, 3% mucus and pigments, 1% fats, and 0.7% inorganic salts.
Lipase	Lipase is an enzyme that catalyzes the breakdown of hydrolysis of fats . Lipases are a subclass of the esterases. Lipases perform essential roles in the digestion, transport and processing of dietary lipids (e.g. triglycerides, fats, oils) in most, if not all, living organisms.
Pepsin	Pepsin is an enzyme whose zymogen (pepsinogen) is released by the chief cells in the stomach and that degrades food proteins into peptides. It was discovered in 1836 by Theodor Schwann who also coined its name from the Greek word pepsis, meaning digestion (peptein: to digest). It was the first enzyme to be discovered, and, in 1929, it became one of the first enzymes to be crystallized, by John H. Northrop.
Secretin	Secretin is a hormone that both controls the environment in the duodenum by regulating secretions of the stomach and pancreas, and regulates water homeostasis throughout the body. It is produced in the S cells of the duodenum, which are located in the crypts of Lieberkühn. In humans, the secretin peptide is encoded by the SCT gene.
Trypsin	Trypsin is a serine protease from the PA clan superfamily, found in the digestive system of many vertebrates, where it hydrolyses proteins. Trypsin is produced in the pancreas as the inactive proenzyme trypsinogen. Trypsin cleaves peptide chains mainly at the carboxyl side of the amino acids lysine or arginine, except when either is followed by proline.
Biofilm	A biofilm is any group of microorganisms in which cells stick to each other on a surface. These adherent cells are frequently embedded within a self-produced matrix of extracellular polymeric substance (EPS). Biofilm EPS, which is also referred to as slime (although not everything described as slime is a biofilm), is a polymeric conglomeration generally composed of extracellular DNA, proteins, and polysaccharides.

2. Energy, Life, and the Biosphere

1. In biology, the _____ is the small portion of an enzyme where substrate molecules bind and undergo a chemical reaction. This chemical reaction occurs when a substrate collides with and slots into the _____ of an enzyme. The _____ is usually found in a 3-D groove or pocket of the enzyme, lined with amino acid residues (or nucleotides in RNA enzymes).

   a. 21-Hydroxylase
   b. -galactosylglucosylceramide N-acetylgalactosaminyltransferase
   c. Methionine synthase
   d. Active site

2. _____ is an enzyme that catalyses the hydrolysis of starch into sugars. _____ is present in the saliva of humans and some other mammals, where it begins the chemical process of digestion. Foods that contain much starch but little sugar, such as rice and potato, taste slightly sweet as they are chewed because _____ turns some of their starch into sugar in the mouth.

   a. Amylase
   b. -galactosylglucosylceramide N-acetylgalactosaminyltransferase
   c. Methionine synthase
   d. 3-Hydroxyaspartic acid

3. A _____ is any group of microorganisms in which cells stick to each other on a surface. These adherent cells are frequently embedded within a self-produced matrix of extracellular polymeric substance (EPS). _____ EPS, which is also referred to as slime (although not everything described as slime is a _____), is a polymeric conglomeration generally composed of extracellular DNA, proteins, and polysaccharides.

   a. Bacterial outer membrane
   b. Biofilm
   c. N-Acetylgalactosamine
   d. N-Acetylglucosamine

4. _____, also known as maltobiose or malt sugar, is a disaccharide formed from two units of glucose joined with an a(1?4) bond, formed from a condensation reaction. The isomer iso_____ has two glucose molecules linked through an a(1?6) bond. _____ is the second member of an important biochemical series of glucose chains.

   a. Cellobiose
   b. Gentiobiose
   c. Kojibiose
   d. Maltose

5. . _____ or gall is a bitter-tasting, dark green to yellowish brown fluid, produced by the liver of most vertebrates, that aids the digestion of lipids in the small intestine. In many species, _____ is stored in the gallbladder and, when the organism eats, is discharged into the duodenum. _____ is 85% water, 10% _____ salts, 3% mucus and pigments, 1% fats, and 0.7% inorganic salts.

a. 6-Monoacetylmorphine
b. Bile
c. Biomolecule
d. DARPin

1. d
2. a
3. b
4. d
5. b

You can take the complete Chapter Practice Test

for 2. Energy, Life, and the Biosphere
on all key terms, persons, places, and concepts.

Online 99 Cents

http://www.JustTheFacts101.com

Use www.JustTheFacts101.com for all your study needs

including Facts101's online interactive problem solving labs in

chemistry, statistics, mathematics, and more.

3. Exchanging Materials with the Environment

CHAPTER OUTLINE: KEY TERMS, PEOPLE, PLACES, CONCEPTS

Hydra

Transport protein

Cell membrane

DNA replication

Glycolipid

Glycoprotein

Lipid

Active transport

Facilitated diffusion

Passive transport

Endocytosis

Cystic fibrosis

Aldosterone

3. Exchanging Materials with the Environment

Hydra	Hydra is a genus of small, simple, fresh-water animals that possess radial symmetry. Hydra are predatory animals belonging to the phylum Cnidaria and the class Hydrozoa. They can be found in most unpolluted fresh-water ponds, lakes, and streams in the temperate and tropical regions and can be found by gently sweeping a collecting net through weedy areas.
Transport protein	A transport protein is a protein which serves the function of moving other materials within an organism. Transport proteins are vital to the growth and life of all living things. There are several different kinds of transport proteins.
Cell membrane	The 'cell membrane' is a biological membrane that separates the interior of all cells from the outside environment. The cell membrane is selectively permeable to ions and organic molecules and controls the movement of substances in and out of cells. The basic function of the cell membrane is to protect the cell from its surroundings.
DNA replication	DNA replication is the process of producing two identical copies from one original DNA molecule. This biological process occurs in all living organisms and is the basis for biological inheritance. DNA is composed of two strands and each strand of the original DNA molecule serves as template for the production of the complementary strand, a process referred to as semiconservative replication.
Glycolipid	Glycolipids are lipids with a carbohydrate attached. Their role is to provide energy and also serve as markers for cellular recognition.
Glycoprotein	Glycoproteins are proteins that contain oligosaccharide chains covalently attached to polypeptide side-chains. The carbohydrate is attached to the protein in a cotranslational or posttranslational modification. This process is known as glycosylation.
Lipid	Lipids are a group of naturally occurring molecules that include fats, waxes, sterols, fat-soluble vitamins, monoglycerides, diglycerides, triglycerides, phospholipids, and others. The main biological functions of lipids include storing energy, signaling, and acting as structural components of cell membranes. Lipids have applications in the cosmetic and food industries as well as in nanotechnology.
Active transport	Active transport is the movement of all types of molecules across a cell membrane against its concentration gradient . In all cells, this is usually concerned with accumulating high concentrations of molecules that the cell needs, such as ions, glucose and amino acids. If the process uses chemical energy, such as from adenosine triphosphate (ATP), it is termed primary active transport.
Facilitated diffusion	Facilitated diffusion is a process of passive transport (as opposed to active transport), with this passive transport aided by integral membrane proteins. Facilitated diffusion is the spontaneous passage of molecules or ions across a biological membrane passing through specific transmembrane integral proteins.

Passive transport	Passive transport is a movement of biochemicals and other atomic or molecular substances across membranes. Unlike active transport, it does not require an input of chemical energy, being driven by the growth of entropy of the system. The rate of passive transport depends on the (semi-) permeability of the cell membrane, which, in turn, depends on the organization and characteristics of the membrane lipids and proteins.
Endocytosis	Endocytosis is an energy-using process by which cells absorb molecules by engulfing them. It is used by all cells of the body because most substances important to them are large polar molecules that cannot pass through the hydrophobic plasma or cell membrane. The process which is the opposite to endocytosis is exocytosis.
Cystic fibrosis	Cystic fibrosis, also known as mucoviscidosis, is an autosomal recessive genetic disorder that affects most critically the lungs, and also the pancreas, liver, and intestine. It is characterized by abnormal transport of chloride and sodium across an epithelium, leading to thick, viscous secretions. The name cystic fibrosis refers to the characteristic scarring (fibrosis) and cyst formation within the pancreas, first recognized in the 1930s.
Aldosterone	Aldosterone is a steroid hormone produced by the outer section (zona glomerulosa) of the adrenal cortex in the adrenal gland. It plays a central role in the regulation of blood pressure mainly by acting on the distal tubules and collecting ducts of the nephron, increasing reabsorption of ions and water in the kidney, to cause the conservation of sodium, secretion of potassium, increased water retention, and increased blood pressure. When dysregulated, aldosterone is pathogenic and contributes to the development and progression of cardiovascular and renal disease.

CHAPTER QUIZ: KEY TERMS, PEOPLE, PLACES, CONCEPTS

1. _____s are lipids with a carbohydrate attached. Their role is to provide energy and also serve as markers for cellular recognition.

    a. Carbohydrate acetalisation
    b. Glycolipid
    c. Disaccharide
    d. Ferrier carbocyclization

2. . _____ is a genus of small, simple, fresh-water animals that possess radial symmetry. _____ are predatory animals belonging to the phylum Cnidaria and the class Hydrozoa. They can be found in most unpolluted fresh-water ponds, lakes, and streams in the temperate and tropical regions and can be found by gently sweeping a collecting net through weedy areas.

a. Barley
b. Bifidobacterium longum
c. Hydra
d. Botryllus schlosseri

3. _____s are proteins that contain oligosaccharide chains covalently attached to polypeptide side-chains. The carbohydrate is attached to the protein in a cotranslational or posttranslational modification. This process is known as glycosylation.

a. Glycoprotein
b. Cyanohydrin reaction
c. Disaccharide
d. Ferrier carbocyclization

4. The '_____' is a biological membrane that separates the interior of all cells from the outside environment. The _____ is selectively permeable to ions and organic molecules and controls the movement of substances in and out of cells. The basic function of the _____ is to protect the cell from its surroundings.

a. Cell membrane
b. Biofilm
c. Biological membrane
d. Calcium 2-aminoethylphosphate

5. A _____ is a protein which serves the function of moving other materials within an organism. _____s are vital to the growth and life of all living things. There are several different kinds of _____s.

a. Membrane transport protein
b. Transport protein
c. Chaconine
d. Glycoalkaloid

1. b
2. c
3. a
4. a
5. b

You can take the complete Chapter Practice Test

for 3. Exchanging Materials with the Environment
on all key terms, persons, places, and concepts.

Online 99 Cents

http://www.JustTheFacts101.com

Use www.JustTheFacts101.com for all your study needs

including Facts101's online interactive problem solving labs in

chemistry, statistics, mathematics, and more.

CHAPTER OUTLINE: KEY TERMS, PEOPLE, PLACES, CONCEPTS

	Stroma
	Thylakoid
	Rhodopsin
	Photosystem
	Transformation

CHAPTER HIGHLIGHTS & NOTES: KEY TERMS, PEOPLE, PLACES, CONCEPTS

Stroma	Stroma, in botany, refers to the colourless fluid surrounding the grana within the chloroplast.
	Within the stroma are grana, stacks of thylakoids, the sub-organelles, where photosynthesis is commenced before the chemical changes are completed in the stroma.
	Photosynthesis occurs in two stages.
Thylakoid	A thylakoid is a membrane-bound compartment inside chloroplasts and cyanobacteria. They are the site of the light-dependent reactions of photosynthesis. Thylakoids consist of a thylakoid membrane surrounding a thylakoid lumen.
Rhodopsin	Rhodopsin, also known as visual purple, is a biological pigment in photoreceptor cells of the retina that is responsible for the first events in the perception of light. Rhodopsins belong to the G-protein-coupled receptor family and are extremely sensitive to light, enabling vision in low-light conditions. Exposed to light, the pigment immediately photobleaches, and it takes about 45 minutes to regenerate fully in humans.
Photosystem	Photosystems are functional and structural units of protein complexes involved in photosynthesis that together carry out the primary photochemistry of photosynthesis: the absorption of light and the transfer of energy and electrons. They are found in the thylakoid membranes of plants, algae and cyanobacteria (in plants and algae these are located in the chloroplasts), or in the cytoplasmic membrane of photosynthetic bacteria.

4. Autotrophy: Collecting Energy from the Nonliving Environment

Transformation	In molecular biology, transformation is genetic alteration of a cell resulting from the direct uptake, incorporation and expression of exogenous genetic material from its surroundings and taken up through the cell membrane(s). Transformation occurs naturally in some species of bacteria, but it can also be effected by artificial means in other cells. For transformation to happen, bacteria must be in a state of competence, which might occur as a time-limited response to environmental conditions such as starvation and cell density.

CHAPTER QUIZ: KEY TERMS, PEOPLE, PLACES, CONCEPTS

1. _____, in botany, refers to the colourless fluid surrounding the grana within the chloroplast.

   Within the _____ are grana, stacks of thylakoids, the sub-organelles, where photosynthesis is commenced before the chemical changes are completed in the _____.

   Photosynthesis occurs in two stages.

   a. Bacterial outer membrane
   b. Biofilm
   c. Stroma
   d. Calcium 2-aminoethylphosphate

2. A _____ is a membrane-bound compartment inside chloroplasts and cyanobacteria. They are the site of the light-dependent reactions of photosynthesis. _____s consist of a _____ membrane surrounding a _____ lumen.

   a. Bacterial outer membrane
   b. Biofilm
   c. Thylakoid
   d. Calcium 2-aminoethylphosphate

3. . _____s are functional and structural units of protein complexes involved in photosynthesis that together carry out the primary photochemistry of photosynthesis: the absorption of light and the transfer of energy and electrons. They are found in the thylakoid membranes of plants, algae and cyanobacteria (in plants and algae these are located in the chloroplasts), or in the cytoplasmic membrane of photosynthetic bacteria.

   a. Bacteriorhodopsin
   b. Bcl-2
   c. Beta-secretase 1

4. _____, also known as visual purple, is a biological pigment in photoreceptor cells of the retina that is responsible for the first events in the perception of light. _____s belong to the G-protein-coupled receptor family and are extremely sensitive to light, enabling vision in low-light conditions. Exposed to light, the pigment immediately photobleaches, and it takes about 45 minutes to regenerate fully in humans.

    a. Biliverdin
    b. Rhodopsin
    c. Boletocrocin
    d. Calostomal

5. In molecular biology, _____ is genetic alteration of a cell resulting from the direct uptake, incorporation and expression of exogenous genetic material from its surroundings and taken up through the cell membrane(s). _____ occurs naturally in some species of bacteria, but it can also be effected by artificial means in other cells. For _____ to happen, bacteria must be in a state of competence, which might occur as a time-limited response to environmental conditions such as starvation and cell density.

    a. Gendicine
    b. Gene delivery
    c. Transformation
    d. Microinjection

1. c
2. c
3. d
4. b
5. c

You can take the complete Chapter Practice Test

for 4. Autotrophy: Collecting Energy from the Nonliving Environment
on all key terms, persons, places, and concepts.

Online 99 Cents

http://www.JustTheFacts101.com

Use www.JustTheFacts101.com for all your study needs

including Facts101's online interactive problem solving labs in

chemistry, statistics, mathematics, and more.

5. Cell Respiration: Releasing Chemical Energy

	Glycolysis
	Cytochrome
	Epinephrine
	Protein
	Leptin

CHAPTER HIGHLIGHTS & NOTES: KEY TERMS, PEOPLE, PLACES, CONCEPTS

Glycolysis	Glycolysis is the metabolic pathway that converts glucose $C_6H_{12}O_6$, into pyruvate, $CH_3COCOO^- + H^+$. The free energy released in this process is used to form the high-energy compounds ATP (adenosine triphosphate) and NADH (reduced nicotinamide adenine dinucleotide).
	Glycolysis does not require or consume oxygen.
Cytochrome	Cytochromes are, in general, membrane-bound hemeproteins containing heme groups and are primarily responsible for the generation of ATP via electron transport.
	They are found either as monomeric proteins (e.g., cytochrome c) or as subunits of bigger enzymatic complexes that catalyze redox reactions.
Epinephrine	Epinephrine is a hormone and a neurotransmitter. Epinephrine has many functions in the body, regulating heart rate, blood vessel and air passage diameters, and metabolic shifts; epinephrine release is a crucial component of the fight-or-flight response of the sympathetic nervous system. In chemical terms, epinephrine is one of a group of monoamines called the catecholamines.
Protein	Proteins are large biological molecules, or macromolecules, consisting of one or more chains of amino acids. Proteins perform a vast array of functions within living organisms, including catalyzing metabolic reactions, replicating DNA, responding to stimuli, and transporting molecules from one location to another. Proteins differ from one another primarily in their sequence of amino acids, which is dictated by the nucleotide sequence of their genes, and which usually results in folding of the protein into a specific three-dimensional structure that determines its activity.

| Leptin | Leptin is a 16-kDa adipokine that plays a key role in regulating energy intake and expenditure, including appetite and hunger, metabolism, and behavior. It is one of the most important adipose-derived hormones. Leptin functions by binding to the leptin receptor. |

1. _____s are, in general, membrane-bound hemeproteins containing heme groups and are primarily responsible for the generation of ATP via electron transport.

    They are found either as monomeric proteins (e.g., _____ c) or as subunits of bigger enzymatic complexes that catalyze redox reactions.

    a. Cytochrome
    b. Sterolin
    c. TAP1
    d. TAP2

2. _____ is the metabolic pathway that converts glucose $C_6H_{12}O_6$, into pyruvate, $CH_3COCOO^- + H^+$. The free energy released in this process is used to form the high-energy compounds ATP (adenosine triphosphate) and NADH (reduced nicotinamide adenine dinucleotide).

    _____ does not require or consume oxygen.

    a. Carbohydrate
    b. Carbohydrate chemistry
    c. Carbohydrate conformation
    d. Glycolysis

3. _____ is a 16-kDa adipokine that plays a key role in regulating energy intake and expenditure, including appetite and hunger, metabolism, and behavior. It is one of the most important adipose-derived hormones. _____ functions by binding to the _____ receptor.

    a. Leptin
    b. Big gastrin
    c. Bovine somatotropin
    d. Bradykinin

4. . _____ is a hormone and a neurotransmitter.

_____ has many functions in the body, regulating heart rate, blood vessel and air passage diameters, and metabolic shifts; _____ release is a crucial component of the fight-or-flight response of the sympathetic nervous system. In chemical terms, _____ is one of a group of monoamines called the catecholamines.

a. Carbidopa
b. Catecholamine
c. Deoxyepinephrine
d. Epinephrine

5. _____s are large biological molecules, or macromolecules, consisting of one or more chains of amino acids. _____s perform a vast array of functions within living organisms, including catalyzing metabolic reactions, replicating DNA, responding to stimuli, and transporting molecules from one location to another. _____s differ from one another primarily in their sequence of amino acids, which is dictated by the nucleotide sequence of their genes, and which usually results in folding of the _____ into a specific three-dimensional structure that determines its activity.

a. Biomarker discovery
b. Protein
c. CASTp
d. Deproteination

1. a
2. d
3. a
4. d
5. b

You can take the complete Chapter Practice Test

for 5. Cell Respiration: Releasing Chemical Energy
on all key terms, persons, places, and concepts.

Online 99 Cents

http://www.JustTheFacts101.com

Use www.JustTheFacts101.com for all your study needs

including Facts101's online interactive problem solving labs in

chemistry, statistics, mathematics, and more.

6. Cell Structures and Their Functions

CHAPTER OUTLINE: KEY TERMS, PEOPLE, PLACES, CONCEPTS

	Plasmid
	Cytoskeleton
	Ribosome
	Vesicle
	Biofilm
	Hydra

CHAPTER HIGHLIGHTS & NOTES: KEY TERMS, PEOPLE, PLACES, CONCEPTS

Plasmid	A plasmid is a small DNA molecule that is physically separate from, and can replicate independently of, chromosomal DNA within a cell. Most commonly found as small circular, double-stranded DNA molecules in bacteria, plasmids are sometimes present in archaea and eukaryotic organisms. In nature, plasmids carry genes that may benefit survival of the organism (e.g. antibiotic resistance), and can frequently be transmitted from one bacterium to another (even of another species) via horizontal gene transfer.
Cytoskeleton	The cytoskeleton is a cellular scaffolding or skeleton contained within a cell's cytoplasm. The cytoskeleton is present in all cells; it was once thought to be unique to eukaryotes, but recent research has identified the prokaryotic cytoskeleton. It forms structures such as flagella, cilia and lamellipodia and plays important roles in both intracellular transport (the movement of vesicles and organelles, for example) and cellular division.
Ribosome	The ribosome is a large and complex molecular machine, found within all living cells, that serves as the primary site of biological protein synthesis (translation). Ribosomes link amino acids together in the order specified by messenger RNA (mRNA) molecules. Ribosomes consist of two major subunits--the small ribosomal subunit reads the mRNA, while the large subunit joins amino acids to form a polypeptide chain.
Vesicle	In cell biology, a vesicle is a small bubble within a cell, and thus a type of organelle. Enclosed by lipid bilayer, vesicles can form naturally, for example, during endocytosis. Alternatively, they may be prepared artificially, in which case they are called liposomes.

6. Cell Structures and Their Functions

Biofilm	A biofilm is any group of microorganisms in which cells stick to each other on a surface. These adherent cells are frequently embedded within a self-produced matrix of extracellular polymeric substance (EPS). Biofilm EPS, which is also referred to as slime (although not everything described as slime is a biofilm), is a polymeric conglomeration generally composed of extracellular DNA, proteins, and polysaccharides.
Hydra	Hydra is a genus of small, simple, fresh-water animals that possess radial symmetry. Hydra are predatory animals belonging to the phylum Cnidaria and the class Hydrozoa. They can be found in most unpolluted fresh-water ponds, lakes, and streams in the temperate and tropical regions and can be found by gently sweeping a collecting net through weedy areas.

1. A _____ is a small DNA molecule that is physically separate from, and can replicate independently of, chromosomal DNA within a cell. Most commonly found as small circular, double-stranded DNA molecules in bacteria, _____s are sometimes present in archaea and eukaryotic organisms. In nature, _____s carry genes that may benefit survival of the organism (e.g. antibiotic resistance), and can frequently be transmitted from one bacterium to another (even of another species) via horizontal gene transfer.

   a. Bacterial artificial chromosome
   b. Bacterial conjugation
   c. Plasmid
   d. Base calling

2. The _____ is a cellular scaffolding or skeleton contained within a cell's cytoplasm. The _____ is present in all cells; it was once thought to be unique to eukaryotes, but recent research has identified the prokaryotic _____. It forms structures such as flagella, cilia and lamellipodia and plays important roles in both intracellular transport (the movement of vesicles and organelles, for example) and cellular division.

   a. 3-Hydroxyaspartic acid
   b. Cytoskeleton
   c. Glycoalkaloid
   d. Solamargine

3. . _____ is a genus of small, simple, fresh-water animals that possess radial symmetry. _____ are predatory animals belonging to the phylum Cnidaria and the class Hydrozoa. They can be found in most unpolluted fresh-water ponds, lakes, and streams in the temperate and tropical regions and can be found by gently sweeping a collecting net through weedy areas.

   a. Barley
   b. Hydra

    c. Bombyx mori

    d. Botryllus schlosseri

4. The _____ is a large and complex molecular machine, found within all living cells, that serves as the primary site of biological protein synthesis (translation). _____s link amino acids together in the order specified by messenger RNA (mRNA) molecules. _____s consist of two major subunits--the small ribosomal subunit reads the mRNA, while the large subunit joins amino acids to form a polypeptide chain.

    a. Chaperone

    b. Ribosome

    c. Foldase

    d. Holdase

5. In cell biology, a _____ is a small bubble within a cell, and thus a type of organelle. Enclosed by lipid bilayer, _____s can form naturally, for example, during endocytosis. Alternatively, they may be prepared artificially, in which case they are called liposomes.

    a. Bacterial outer membrane

    b. Biofilm

    c. Vesicle

    d. Calcium 2-aminoethylphosphate

1. c
2. b
3. b
4. b
5. c

___

You can take the complete Chapter Practice Test

for 6. Cell Structures and Their Functions
on all key terms, persons, places, and concepts.

Online 99 Cents

http://www.JustTheFacts101.com

Use www.JustTheFacts101.com for all your study needs

including Facts101's online interactive problem solving labs in

chemistry, statistics, mathematics, and more.

7. Transport Systems

	Nutrient
	Myosin
	Hemoglobin
	Platelet
	Coagulation
	Fibrin
	Fibrinogen
	Epidermal growth factor
	Growth factor

CHAPTER HIGHLIGHTS & NOTES: KEY TERMS, PEOPLE, PLACES, CONCEPTS

Nutrient	A nutrient is a chemical that an organism needs to live and grow or a substance used in an organism's metabolism which must be taken in from its environment. They are used to build and repair tissues, regulate body processes and are converted to and used as energy. Methods for nutrient intake vary, with animals and protists consuming foods that are digested by an internal digestive system, but most plants ingest nutrients directly from the soil through their roots or from the atmosphere.
Myosin	Myosins comprise a family of ATP-dependent motor proteins and are best known for their role in muscle contraction and their involvement in a wide range of other eukaryotic motility processes. They are responsible for actin-based motility. The term was originally used to describe a group of similar ATPases found in striated and smooth muscle cells.
Hemoglobin	Haemoglobin ; also spelled hemoglobin and abbreviated Hb or Hgb, is the iron-containing oxygen-transport metalloprotein in the red blood cells of all vertebrates as well as the tissues of some invertebrates. Hemoglobin in the blood carries oxygen from the respiratory organs (lungs or gills) to the rest of the body (i.e.

the tissues) where it releases the oxygen to burn nutrients to provide energy to power the functions of the organism, and collects the resultant carbon dioxide to bring it back to the respiratory organs to be dispensed from the organism.

In mammals, the protein makes up about 97% of the red blood cells' dry content (by weight), and around 35% of the total content (including water).

Platelet	Platelets, or thrombocytes, are small, disk shaped clear cell fragments (i.e. cells that do not have a nucleus), 2-3 μm in diameter, which are derived from fragmentation of precursor megakaryocytes. The average lifespan of a platelet is normally just 5 to 9 days. Platelets are a natural source of growth factors.
Coagulation	Coagulation is the process by which blood forms clots. It is an important part of hemostasis, the cessation of blood loss from a damaged vessel, wherein a damaged blood vessel wall is covered by a platelet and fibrin-containing clot to stop bleeding and begin repair of the damaged vessel. Disorders of coagulation can lead to an increased risk of bleeding (hemorrhage) or obstructive clotting (thrombosis).
Fibrin	Fibrin is a fibrous, non-globular protein involved in the clotting of blood. It is formed from fibrinogen by the protease thrombin, and is then polymerised to form a 'mesh' that forms a hemostatic plug or clot (in conjunction with platelets) over a wound site.
	Fibrin is involved in signal transduction, blood coagulation, and platelet activation.
Fibrinogen	Fibrinogen is a soluble, 340 kDa plasma glycoprotein, that is converted by thrombin into fibrin during blood clot formation. Fibrinogen is synthesized in the liver by the hepatocytes. The concentration of fibrin in the blood plasma is 200-400 mg/dL (normally measured using the Clauss method).
Epidermal growth factor	Epidermal growth factor is a growth factor that stimulates cell growth, proliferation, and differentiation by binding to its receptor EGFR. Human Epidermal growth factor is a 6045-Da protein with 53 amino acid residues and three intramolecular disulfide bonds.
Growth factor	A growth factor is a naturally occurring substance capable of stimulating cellular growth, proliferation and cellular differentiation. Usually it is a protein or a steroid hormone. Growth factors are important for regulating a variety of cellular processes.

7. Transport Systems

1. Haemoglobin ; also spelled _____ and abbreviated Hb or Hgb, is the iron-containing oxygen-transport metalloprotein in the red blood cells of all vertebrates as well as the tissues of some invertebrates. _____ in the blood carries oxygen from the respiratory organs (lungs or gills) to the rest of the body (i.e. the tissues) where it releases the oxygen to burn nutrients to provide energy to power the functions of the organism, and collects the resultant carbon dioxide to bring it back to the respiratory organs to be dispensed from the organism.

   In mammals, the protein makes up about 97% of the red blood cells' dry content (by weight), and around 35% of the total content (including water).

   a. Carboxyhemoglobin
   b. Fetal hemoglobin
   c. Glycated hemoglobin
   d. Hemoglobin

2. _____s, or thrombocytes, are small, disk shaped clear cell fragments (i.e. cells that do not have a nucleus), 2-3 μm in diameter, which are derived from fragmentation of precursor megakaryocytes. The average lifespan of a _____ is normally just 5 to 9 days. _____s are a natural source of growth factors.

   a. Platelet
   b. Clot retraction
   c. Coagulation
   d. Cofact

3. _____ is a fibrous, non-globular protein involved in the clotting of blood. It is formed from fibrinogen by the protease thrombin, and is then polymerised to form a 'mesh' that forms a hemostatic plug or clot (in conjunction with platelets) over a wound site.

   _____ is involved in signal transduction, blood coagulation, and platelet activation.

   a. Ceruloplasmin
   b. C-reactive protein
   c. Ferritin
   d. Fibrin

4. _____s comprise a family of ATP-dependent motor proteins and are best known for their role in muscle contraction and their involvement in a wide range of other eukaryotic motility processes. They are responsible for actin-based motility. The term was originally used to describe a group of similar ATPases found in striated and smooth muscle cells.

   a. Myosin
   b. Crescentin
   c. Cytoskeleton
   d. Filopodia

5. _____ is a growth factor that stimulates cell growth, proliferation, and differentiation by binding to its receptor EGFR. Human _____ is a 6045-Da protein with 53 amino acid residues and three intramolecular disulfide bonds.

    a. Basic fibroblast growth factor

    b. Epidermal growth factor

    c. CCN intercellular signaling protein

    d. CTGF

1. d
2. a
3. d
4. a
5. b

You can take the complete Chapter Practice Test

for 7. Transport Systems
on all key terms, persons, places, and concepts.

Online 99 Cents

http://www.JustTheFacts101.com

Use www.JustTheFacts101.com for all your study needs

including Facts101's online interactive problem solving labs in

chemistry, statistics, mathematics, and more.

8. The Cell Cycle

CHAPTER OUTLINE: KEY TERMS, PEOPLE, PLACES, CONCEPTS

	Cell division
	DNA polymerase
	Replisome
	Semiconservative replication
	Chromatin
	Nucleosome
	Excision repair
	Chromatid
	Sister chromatids
	Microtubule
	Cyclin

CHAPTER HIGHLIGHTS & NOTES: KEY TERMS, PEOPLE, PLACES, CONCEPTS

Cell division	Cell division is the process by which a parent cell divides into two or more daughter cells. Cell division usually occurs as part of a larger cell cycle. In eukaryotes, there are two distinct type of cell division: a vegetative division, whereby each daughter cell is genetically identical to the parent cell (mitosis), and a reductive cell division, whereby the number of chromosomes in the daughter cells is reduced by half, to produce haploid gametes (meiosis).
DNA polymerase	A DNA polymerase is a cellular or viral polymerase enzyme that synthesizes DNA molecules from their nucleotide building blocks. DNA polymerases are essential for DNA replication, and usually function in pairs while copying one double-stranded DNA molecule into two double-stranded DNAs in a process termed semiconservative DNA replication.

8. The Cell Cycle

Replisome	The replisome is a complex molecular machine that carries out replication of DNA. The replisome first unwinds double stranded DNA into two single strands. For each of the resulting single strands, a new complementary sequence of DNA is synthesized. The net result is formation of two new double stranded DNA sequences that are exact copies of the original double stranded DNA sequence.
Semiconservative replication	Semiconservative replication describes the mechanism by which DNA is replicated in all known cells. This mechanism of replication was one of three models originally proposed for DNA replication:•Semiconservative replication would produce two copies that each contained one of the original strands and one new strand.•Conservative replication would leave the two original template DNA strands together in a double helix and would produce a copy composed of two new strands containing all of the new DNA base pairs.•Dispersive replication would produce two copies of the DNA, both containing distinct regions of DNA composed of either both original strands or both new strands. The deciphering of the structure of DNA by Watson and Crick in 1953 suggested that each strand of the double helix would serve as a template for synthesis of a new strand. However, there was no way of knowing how the newly synthesized strands might combine with the template strands to form two double helical DNA molecules.
Chromatin	Chromatin is the combination of DNA and proteins that make up the contents of the nucleus of a cell. The primary functions of chromatin are 1) to package DNA into a smaller volume to fit in the cell, 2) to strengthen the DNA to allow mitosis, 3) to prevent DNA damage, and 4) to control gene expression and DNA replication. The primary protein components of chromatin are histones that compact the DNA. Chromatin is only found in eukaryotic cells: prokaryotic cells have a very different organization of their DNA which is referred to as a genophore (a chromosome without chromatin).
Nucleosome	A nucleosome is the basic unit of DNA packaging in eukaryotes, consisting of a segment of DNA wound in sequence around eight histone protein cores. This structure is often compared to thread wrapped around a spool. Nucleosomes form the fundamental repeating units of eukaryotic chromatin, which is used to pack the large eukaryotic genomes into the nucleus while still ensuring appropriate access to it (in mammalian cells approximately 2 m of linear DNA have to be packed into a nucleus of roughly 10 μm diameter).
Excision repair	Excision repair is a term applied to several DNA repair mechanisms. They remove the damaged nucleotides and are able to determine the correct sequence from the complementary strand of DNA.

	Specific mechanisms include:•Base excision repair which repairs damage due to a single nucleotide caused by oxidation, alkylation, hydrolysis, or deamination;•Nucleotide excision repair which repairs damage affecting 2-30 nucleotide-length strands. These include bulky, helix distorting damage, such as thymine dimerization and other types of cyclobutyl dimerization caused by UV light as well as single-strand breaks.
Chromatid	A chromatid is one copy of a duplicated chromosome, which generally is joined to the other copy by a centromere, for the process of nuclear division . They are normally identical ('homozygous') but may have slight differences in the case of mutations, in which case they are heterozygous. They are called sister chromatids so long as they are joined by the centromeres.
Sister chromatids	Sister chromatids are generated when a single chromosome is replicated into two copies of itself, these copies being called sister chromatids. Compare sister chromatids to homologous chromosomes, which are the two different copies of a chromosome that diploid organisms (like humans) inherit, one from each parent. In other words, while sister chromatids are by and large identical (since they carry the same alleles, also called variants or versions, of genes) because they derive from one original chromosome, homologous chromosomes might or might not be the same as each other because they derive from different parents.
Microtubule	Microtubules are a component of the cytoskeleton, found throughout the cytoplasm. These tubular polymers of tubulin can grow as long as 50 micrometres, with an average length of 25 μm and are highly dynamic. The outer diameter of a microtubule is about 25 nm while the inner diameter is about 12 nm.
Cyclin	Cyclins are a family of proteins that control the progression of cells through the cell cycle by activating cyclin-dependent kinase enzymes.

8. The Cell Cycle

1. _____ describes the mechanism by which DNA is replicated in all known cells. This mechanism of replication was one of three models originally proposed for DNA replication:•_____ would produce two copies that each contained one of the original strands and one new strand.•Conservative replication would leave the two original template DNA strands together in a double helix and would produce a copy composed of two new strands containing all of the new DNA base pairs.•Dispersive replication would produce two copies of the DNA, both containing distinct regions of DNA composed of either both original strands or both new strands.

   The deciphering of the structure of DNA by Watson and Crick in 1953 suggested that each strand of the double helix would serve as a template for synthesis of a new strand. However, there was no way of knowing how the newly synthesized strands might combine with the template strands to form two double helical DNA molecules.

   a. DNA clamp
   b. DNA polymerase eta
   c. Semiconservative replication
   d. DNA replication factor CDT1

2. _____ is a term applied to several DNA repair mechanisms. They remove the damaged nucleotides and are able to determine the correct sequence from the complementary strand of DNA.

   Specific mechanisms include:•Base _____ which repairs damage due to a single nucleotide caused by oxidation, alkylation, hydrolysis, or deamination;•Nucleotide _____ which repairs damage affecting 2-30 nucleotide-length strands. These include bulky, helix distorting damage, such as thymine dimerization and other types of cyclobutyl dimerization caused by UV light as well as single-strand breaks.

   a. Base excision repair
   b. DNA glycosylase
   c. DNA mismatch repair
   d. Excision repair

3. _____ are generated when a single chromosome is replicated into two copies of itself, these copies being called _____. Compare _____ to homologous chromosomes, which are the two different copies of a chromosome that diploid organisms (like humans) inherit, one from each parent. In other words, while _____ are by and large identical (since they carry the same alleles, also called variants or versions, of genes) because they derive from one original chromosome, homologous chromosomes might or might not be the same as each other because they derive from different parents.

   a. Bacterial one-hybrid system
   b. Baek Sung-hee
   c. Sister chromatids
   d. BioScale Inc.

4. . _____ is the combination of DNA and proteins that make up the contents of the nucleus of a cell.

The primary functions of _____ are 1) to package DNA into a smaller volume to fit in the cell, 2) to strengthen the DNA to allow mitosis, 3) to prevent DNA damage, and 4) to control gene expression and DNA replication. The primary protein components of _____ are histones that compact the DNA. _____ is only found in eukaryotic cells: prokaryotic cells have a very different organization of their DNA which is referred to as a genophore (a chromosome without _____).

a. Bacterial one-hybrid system
b. Baek Sung-hee
c. Biopunk
d. Chromatin

5. The _____ is a complex molecular machine that carries out replication of DNA. The _____ first unwinds double stranded DNA into two single strands. For each of the resulting single strands, a new complementary sequence of DNA is synthesized. The net result is formation of two new double stranded DNA sequences that are exact copies of the original double stranded DNA sequence.

a. Replisome
b. DNA polymerase eta
c. DNA replication
d. DNA replication factor CDT1

1. c
2. d
3. c
4. d
5. a

You can take the complete Chapter Practice Test

for 8. The Cell Cycle
on all key terms, persons, places, and concepts.

Online 99 Cents

http://www.JustTheFacts101.com

Use www.JustTheFacts101.com for all your study needs

including Facts101's online interactive problem solving labs in

chemistry, statistics, mathematics, and more.

9. Expressing Genetic Information

CHAPTER OUTLINE: KEY TERMS, PEOPLE, PLACES, CONCEPTS

Gene expression

Genetic code

Messenger RNA

Transcription

Transfer RNA

Collagen

DNA replication

Enzyme

Keratin

Hormone

Insulin

Exon

Intron

Ribosome

Reading frame

Ebola virus

9. Expressing Genetic Information

Gene expression	Gene expression is the process by which information from a gene is used in the synthesis of a functional gene product. These products are often proteins, but in non-protein coding genes such as ribosomal RNA (rRNA), transfer RNA (tRNA) or small nuclear RNA (snRNA) genes, the product is a functional RNA. The process of gene expression is used by all known life - eukaryotes (including multicellular organisms), prokaryotes (bacteria and archaea), possibly induced by viruses - to generate the macromolecular machinery for life. Several steps in the gene expression process may be modulated, including the transcription, RNA splicing, translation, and post-translational modification of a protein.
Genetic code	The genetic code is the set of rules by which information encoded within genetic material is translated into proteins by living cells. Biological decoding is accomplished by the ribosome, which links amino acids in an order specified by mRNA, using transfer RNA (tRNA) molecules to carry amino acids and to read the mRNA three nucleotides at a time. The genetic code is highly similar among all organisms and can be expressed in a simple table with 64 entries.
Messenger RNA	Messenger RNA is a large family of RNA molecules that convey genetic information from DNA to the ribosome, where they specify the amino acid sequence of the protein products of gene expression. Following transcription of mRNA by RNA polymerase, the mRNA is translated into a polymer of amino acids: a protein, as summarized in the central dogma of molecular biology. As in DNA, mRNA genetic information is encoded in the sequence of nucleotides, which are arranged into codons consisting of three bases each.
Transcription	Transcription is the first step of gene expression, in which a particular segment of DNA is copied into RNA by the enzyme, RNA polymerase. Both RNA and DNA are nucleic acids, which use base pairs of nucleotides as a complementary language that can be converted back and forth from DNA to RNA by the action of the correct enzymes. During transcription, a DNA sequence is read by an RNA polymerase, which produces a complementary, antiparallel RNA strand.
Transfer RNA	A Transfer RNA is an adaptor molecule composed of RNA, typically 73 to 94 nucleotides in length, that serves as the physical link between the nucleotide sequence of nucleic acids (DNA and RNA) and the amino acid sequence of proteins. It does this by carrying an amino acid to the protein synthetic machinery of a cell (ribosome) as directed by a three-nucleotide sequence (codon) in a messenger RNA (mRNA). As such, tRNAs are a necessary component of protein translation, the biological synthesis of new proteins according to the genetic code.
Collagen	Collagen is the main structural protein of the various connective tissues, in animals. (The name collagen comes from the Greek kolla meaning glue and suffix -gen denoting producing. As the main component of connective tissue, it is the most abundant protein in mammals, making up from 25% to 35% of the whole-body protein content.
DNA replication	DNA replication is the process of producing two identical copies from one original DNA molecule.

9. Expressing Genetic Information

	This biological process occurs in all living organisms and is the basis for biological inheritance. DNA is composed of two strands and each strand of the original DNA molecule serves as template for the production of the complementary strand, a process referred to as semiconservative replication.
Enzyme	Enzymes are large biological molecules responsible for the thousands of metabolic processes that sustain life. They are highly selective catalysts, greatly accelerating both the rate and specificity of metabolic reactions, from the digestion of food to the synthesis of DNA. Most enzymes are proteins, although some catalytic RNA molecules have been identified. Enzymes adopt a specific three-dimensional structure, and may employ organic (e.g. biotin) and inorganic (e.g. magnesium ion) cofactors to assist in catalysis.
Keratin	Keratin is a family of fibrous structural proteins. Keratin is the key structural material making up the outer layer of human skin. It is also the key structural component of hair and nails.
Hormone	A hormone is a chemical released by a cell, a gland, or an organ in one part of the body that affects cells in other parts of the organism. Generally, only a small amount of hormone is required to alter cell metabolism. In essence, it is a chemical messenger that transports a signal from one cell to another.
Insulin	Insulin is a peptide hormone, produced by beta cells of the pancreas, and is central to regulating carbohydrate and fat metabolism in the body. Insulin causes cells in the liver, skeletal muscles, and fat tissue to absorb glucose from the blood. In the liver and skeletal muscles, glucose is stored as glycogen, and in fat cells (adipocytes) it is stored as triglycerides.
Exon	An exon is any nucleotide sequence encoded by a gene that remains present within the final mature RNA product of that gene after introns have been removed by RNA splicing. The term exon refers to both the DNA sequence within a gene and to the corresponding sequence in RNA transcripts. In RNA splicing, introns are removed and exons are covalently joined to one another as part of generating the mature messenger RNA or noncoding RNA product of a gene.
Intron	An intron is any nucleotide sequence within a gene that is removed by RNA splicing while the final mature RNA product of a gene is being generated. The term intron refers to both the DNA sequence within a gene and the corresponding sequence in RNA transcripts. Sequences that are joined together in the final mature RNA after RNA splicing are exons.
Ribosome	The ribosome is a large and complex molecular machine, found within all living cells, that serves as the primary site of biological protein synthesis (translation). Ribosomes link amino acids together in the order specified by messenger RNA (mRNA) molecules. Ribosomes consist of two major subunits--the small ribosomal subunit reads the mRNA, while the large subunit joins amino acids to form a polypeptide chain.

Reading frame	In molecular biology, a reading frame is a way of dividing the sequence of nucleotides in a nucleic acid molecule into a set of consecutive, non-overlapping triplets. Where these triplets equate to amino acids or stop signals during translation, they are called codons.
	A single strand of a nucleic acid molecule has a phosphoryl end, (called the 5'-end) and a hydroxyl, or (3'-end).
Ebola virus	Ebola virus causes an extremely severe disease in humans and in nonhuman primates in the form of viral hemorrhagic fever. EBOV is a select agent, World Health Organization Risk Group 4 Pathogen (requiring Biosafety Level 4-equivalent containment), National Institutes of Health/National Institute of Allergy and Infectious Diseases Category A Priority Pathogen, Centers for Disease Control and Prevention Category A Bioterrorism Agent, and listed as a Biological Agent for Export Control by the Australia Group.

CHAPTER QUIZ: KEY TERMS, PEOPLE, PLACES, CONCEPTS

1. _____ is the process by which information from a gene is used in the synthesis of a functional gene product. These products are often proteins, but in non-protein coding genes such as ribosomal RNA (rRNA), transfer RNA (tRNA) or small nuclear RNA (snRNA) genes, the product is a functional RNA. The process of _____ is used by all known life - eukaryotes (including multicellular organisms), prokaryotes (bacteria and archaea), possibly induced by viruses - to generate the macromolecular machinery for life. Several steps in the _____ process may be modulated, including the transcription, RNA splicing, translation, and post-translational modification of a protein.

   a. Bacterial artificial chromosome
   b. Bacterial conjugation
   c. BamHI
   d. Gene expression

2. _____ causes an extremely severe disease in humans and in nonhuman primates in the form of viral hemorrhagic fever. EBOV is a select agent, World Health Organization Risk Group 4 Pathogen (requiring Biosafety Level 4-equivalent containment), National Institutes of Health/National Institute of Allergy and Infectious Diseases Category A Priority Pathogen, Centers for Disease Control and Prevention Category A Bioterrorism Agent, and listed as a Biological Agent for Export Control by the Australia Group.

   a. Ebola virus
   b. Shiga toxin
   c. Shiga-like toxin
   d. Cystic fibrosis transmembrane conductance regulator

9. Expressing Genetic Information

3. _____ is the main structural protein of the various connective tissues, in animals. (The name _____ comes from the Greek kolla meaning glue and suffix -gen denoting producing. As the main component of connective tissue, it is the most abundant protein in mammals, making up from 25% to 35% of the whole-body protein content.

   a. CD11a
   b. Macrophage-1 antigen
   c. 3-Hydroxyaspartic acid
   d. Collagen

4. _____ is a family of fibrous structural proteins. _____ is the key structural material making up the outer layer of human skin. It is also the key structural component of hair and nails.

   a. Keratin
   b. Crescentin
   c. Cytoskeleton
   d. Filopodia

5. _____ is the first step of gene expression, in which a particular segment of DNA is copied into RNA by the enzyme, RNA polymerase. Both RNA and DNA are nucleic acids, which use base pairs of nucleotides as a complementary language that can be converted back and forth from DNA to RNA by the action of the correct enzymes. During _____, a DNA sequence is read by an RNA polymerase, which produces a complementary, antiparallel RNA strand.

   a. Transcription
   b. C1QL1
   c. CAG promoter
   d. Capping enzyme

1. d

2. a

3. d

4. a

5. a

You can take the complete Chapter Practice Test

for 9. Expressing Genetic Information
on all key terms, persons, places, and concepts.

Online 99 Cents

http://www.JustTheFacts101.com

Use www.JustTheFacts101.com for all your study needs

including Facts101's online interactive problem solving labs in

chemistry, statistics, mathematics, and more.

CHAPTER OUTLINE: KEY TERMS, PEOPLE, PLACES, CONCEPTS

	Keratin
	Cell division
	Homeobox
	Hox gene
	Cholinesterase

CHAPTER HIGHLIGHTS & NOTES: KEY TERMS, PEOPLE, PLACES, CONCEPTS

Keratin	Keratin is a family of fibrous structural proteins. Keratin is the key structural material making up the outer layer of human skin. It is also the key structural component of hair and nails.
Cell division	Cell division is the process by which a parent cell divides into two or more daughter cells. Cell division usually occurs as part of a larger cell cycle. In eukaryotes, there are two distinct type of cell division: a vegetative division, whereby each daughter cell is genetically identical to the parent cell (mitosis), and a reductive cell division, whereby the number of chromosomes in the daughter cells is reduced by half, to produce haploid gametes (meiosis).
Homeobox	A homeobox is a DNA sequence found within genes that are involved in the regulation of patterns of anatomical development in animals, fungi and plants.
Hox gene	Hox genes are a group of related genes that control the body plan of the embryo along the anterior-posterior (head-tail) axis. After the embryonic segments have formed, the Hox proteins determine the type of segment structures (e.g. legs, antennae, and wings in fruit flies or the different vertebrate ribs in humans) that will form on a given segment. Hox proteins thus confer segmental identity, but do not form the actual segments themselves

Hox genes are defined as having the following properties:•their protein product is a transcription factor•they contain a DNA sequence known as the homeobox•in many animals, the organization of the Hox genes on the chromosome is the same as the order of their expression along the anterior-posterior axis of the developing animal, and are thus said to display colinearity.. |

10. Animal Growth and Development

1. _____s are a group of related genes that control the body plan of the embryo along the anterior-posterior (head-tail) axis. After the embryonic segments have formed, the Hox proteins determine the type of segment structures (e.g. legs, antennae, and wings in fruit flies or the different vertebrate ribs in humans) that will form on a given segment. Hox proteins thus confer segmental identity, but do not form the actual segments themselves

    _____s are defined as having the following properties:•their protein product is a transcription factor•they contain a DNA sequence known as the homeobox•in many animals, the organization of the _____s on the chromosome is the same as the order of their expression along the anterior-posterior axis of the developing animal, and are thus said to display colinearity..

    a. BMPR2
    b. Bone morphogenetic protein 1
    c. Hox gene
    d. Bone morphogenetic protein 15

2. _____ is a family of fibrous structural proteins. _____ is the key structural material making up the outer layer of human skin. It is also the key structural component of hair and nails.

    a. Keratin
    b. Crescentin
    c. Cytoskeleton
    d. Filopodia

3. In biochemistry, _____ is a family of enzymes that catalyze the hydrolysis of the neurotransmitter acetylcholine into choline and acetic acid, a reaction necessary to allow a cholinergic neuron to return to its resting state after activation.

    a. 5-lipoxygenase-activating protein
    b. B7
    c. Cholinesterase
    d. BAR domain

4. _____ is the process by which a parent cell divides into two or more daughter cells. _____ usually occurs as part of a larger cell cycle. In eukaryotes, there are two distinct type of _____: a vegetative division, whereby each daughter cell is genetically identical to the parent cell (mitosis), and a reductive _____, whereby the number of chromosomes in the daughter cells is reduced by half, to produce haploid gametes (meiosis).

    a. Cell division
    b. Shiga toxin
    c. Shiga-like toxin
    d. Cystic fibrosis transmembrane conductance regulator

5. . A _____ is a DNA sequence found within genes that are involved in the regulation of patterns of anatomical development in animals, fungi and plants.

a. BACH1
b. Homeobox
c. BATF
d. BAZ1B

1. c

2. a

3. c

4. a

5. b

You can take the complete Chapter Practice Test

for 10. Animal Growth and Development
on all key terms, persons, places, and concepts.

Online 99 Cents

http://www.JustTheFacts101.com

Use www.JustTheFacts101.com for all your study needs

including Facts101's online interactive problem solving labs in

chemistry, statistics, mathematics, and more.

CHAPTER OUTLINE: KEY TERMS, PEOPLE, PLACES, CONCEPTS

	Cytokinin	
	Gibberellin	
	Abscisic acid	
	Ethylene	
	Protoplast	
	Phytochrome	

CHAPTER HIGHLIGHTS & NOTES: KEY TERMS, PEOPLE, PLACES, CONCEPTS

Cytokinin	Cytokinins are a class of plant growth substances (phytohormones) that promote cell division, or cytokinesis, in plant roots and shoots. They are involved primarily in cell growth and differentiation, but also affect apical dominance, axillary bud growth, and leaf senescence. Folke Skoog discovered their effects using coconut milk in the 1940s at the University of Wisconsin-Madison.
Gibberellin	Gibberellins are plant hormones that regulate growth and influence various developmental processes, including stem elongation, germination, dormancy, flowering, sex expression, enzyme induction, and leaf and fruit senescence.

Gibberellin was first recognized in 1926 by a Japanese scientist, Eiichi Kurosawa, studying bakanae, the 'foolish seedling' disease in rice. It was first isolated in 1935 by Teijiro Yabuta and Sumuki, from fungal strains (Gibberella fujikuroi) provided by Kurosawa. |
Abscisic acid	Abscisic acid, also known as abscisin II and dormin, is a plant hormone. ABA functions in many plant developmental processes, including bud dormancy. It is degraded by the enzyme (+)-abscisic acid 8'-hydroxylase into phaseic acid.
Ethylene	Ethylene is a hydrocarbon with the formula C2H4 or $H_2C=CH_2$. It is a colorless flammable gas with a faint 'sweet and musky' odor when pure. It is the simplest alkene (a hydrocarbon with carbon-carbon double bonds), and the simplest unsaturated hydrocarbon after acetylene (C2H2).
Protoplast	Protoplast, from the ancient Greek p??t?? + verb p???? or p??tt? (to mould: deriv. plastic), initially referred to the first organized body of a species.

11. Plant Growth and Development

CHAPTER HIGHLIGHTS & NOTES: KEY TERMS, PEOPLE, PLACES, CONCEPTS

Phytochrome	Phytochrome is a photoreceptor, a pigment that plants use to detect light. It is sensitive to light in the red and far-red region of the visible spectrum. Many flowering plants use it to regulate the time of flowering based on the length of day and night (photoperiodism) and to set circadian rhythms.

CHAPTER QUIZ: KEY TERMS, PEOPLE, PLACES, CONCEPTS

1. _____ is a hydrocarbon with the formula C2H4 or $H_2C=CH_2$. It is a colorless flammable gas with a faint 'sweet and musky' odor when pure. It is the simplest alkene (a hydrocarbon with carbon-carbon double bonds), and the simplest unsaturated hydrocarbon after acetylene (C2H2).

   a. Ethylene
   b. Plant hormone
   c. 1918 flu pandemic
   d. John Martin Poyer

2. _____s are a class of plant growth substances (phytohormones) that promote cell division, or cytokinesis, in plant roots and shoots. They are involved primarily in cell growth and differentiation, but also affect apical dominance, axillary bud growth, and leaf senescence. Folke Skoog discovered their effects using coconut milk in the 1940s at the University of Wisconsin-Madison.

   a. Plant hormone
   b. Cytokinin
   c. John Martin Poyer
   d. RMS Tahiti

3. _____s are plant hormones that regulate growth and influence various developmental processes, including stem elongation, germination, dormancy, flowering, sex expression, enzyme induction, and leaf and fruit senescence.

   _____ was first recognized in 1926 by a Japanese scientist, Eiichi Kurosawa, studying bakanae, the 'foolish seedling' disease in rice. It was first isolated in 1935 by Teijiro Yabuta and Sumuki, from fungal strains (Gibberella fujikuroi) provided by Kurosawa.

   a. 10-Deacetylbaccatin
   b. Gibberellin
   c. Cafestol
   d. Cembrene A

4. . _____, also known as abscisin II and dormin, is a plant hormone.

ABA functions in many plant developmental processes, including bud dormancy. It is degraded by the enzyme (+)-_____ 8'-hydroxylase into phaseic acid.

a. Abscisic acid
b. 1918 flu pandemic
c. John Martin Poyer
d. RMS Tahiti

5. _____, from the ancient Greek p??t?? + verb p???? or p??tt? (to mould: deriv. plastic), initially referred to the first organized body of a species.

_____ has several biological definitions:•A _____ is a plant, bacterial or fungal cell that had its cell wall completely or partially removed using either mechanical or enzymatic means.•_____s: Have their cell wall entirely removed•Spheroplasts: Have their cell wall only partially removed•More generally _____ refers to that unit of biology which is composed of a cell's nucleus and the surrounding protoplasmic materials..

a. Bacterial outer membrane
b. Biofilm
c. Biological membrane
d. Protoplast

1. a
2. b
3. b
4. a
5. d

You can take the complete Chapter Practice Test

for 11. Plant Growth and Development
on all key terms, persons, places, and concepts.

Online 99 Cents

http://www.JustTheFacts101.com

Use www.JustTheFacts101.com for all your study needs

including Facts101's online interactive problem solving labs in

chemistry, statistics, mathematics, and more.

12. Reproduction

	Cell division
	Meiosis
	Cloning
	Follicle-stimulating hormone
	Luteinizing hormone
	Progesterone
	Human chorionic gonadotropin
	Oxytocin

CHAPTER HIGHLIGHTS & NOTES: KEY TERMS, PEOPLE, PLACES, CONCEPTS

Cell division

Cell division is the process by which a parent cell divides into two or more daughter cells. Cell division usually occurs as part of a larger cell cycle. In eukaryotes, there are two distinct type of cell division: a vegetative division, whereby each daughter cell is genetically identical to the parent cell (mitosis), and a reductive cell division, whereby the number of chromosomes in the daughter cells is reduced by half, to produce haploid gametes (meiosis).

Meiosis

Meiosis is a special type of cell division necessary for sexual reproduction in eukaryotes, such as animals, plants and fungi. The number of sets of chromosomes in the cell undergoing meiosis is reduced to half the original number, typically from two sets (diploid) to one set (haploid). The cells produced by meiosis are either gametes (the usual case in animals) or otherwise usually spores from which gametes are ultimately produced (the case in land plants).

Cloning

In biology, cloning is the process of producing similar populations of genetically identical individuals that occurs in nature when organisms such as bacteria, insects or plants reproduce asexually. Cloning in biotechnology refers to processes used to create copies of DNA fragments (molecular cloning), cells (cell cloning), or organisms. The term also refers to the production of multiple copies of a product such as digital media or software.

Follicle-stimulating hormone	Follicle-stimulating hormone is a hormone found in humans and other animals. It is synthesized and secreted by gonadotrophs of the anterior pituitary gland. Follicle stimulating hormone regulates the development, growth, pubertal maturation, and reproductive processes of the body.
Luteinizing hormone	Luteinizing hormone is a hormone produced by gonadotroph cells in the anterior pituitary gland. In females, an acute rise of LH ('LH surge') triggers ovulation and development of the corpus luteum. In males, where LH had also been called interstitial cell-stimulating hormone (ICSH), it stimulates Leydig cell production of testosterone.
Progesterone	Progesterone also known as P4 is a C-21 steroid hormone involved in the female menstrual cycle, pregnancy (supports gestation) and embryogenesis of humans and other species. Progesterone belongs to a class of hormones called progestogens, and is the major naturally occurring human progestogen.
Human chorionic gonadotropin	In molecular biology, human chorionic gonadotropin is a hormone produced by the syncytiotrophoblast, a component of the fertilized egg, after conception. Following implantation, the syncytiotrophoblast gives rise to the placenta. Some cancerous tumors produce this hormone; therefore, elevated levels measured when the patient is not pregnant can lead to a cancer diagnosis.
Oxytocin	Oxytocin is a mammalian neurohypophysial hormone, (secreted by the posterior pituitary gland), that acts primarily as a neuromodulator in the brain.
	Oxytocin plays roles in sexual reproduction, in particular during and after childbirth. It is released in large amounts after distension of the cervix and uterus during labor, facilitating birth, maternal bonding, and, after stimulation of the nipples, lactation.

1. _____ is a hormone produced by gonadotroph cells in the anterior pituitary gland. In females, an acute rise of LH ('LH surge') triggers ovulation and development of the corpus luteum. In males, where LH had also been called interstitial cell-stimulating hormone (ICSH), it stimulates Leydig cell production of testosterone.

    a. CD1D
    b. CD32B
    c. Luteinizing hormone
    d. Dog leukocyte antigen

2. . _____ is the process by which a parent cell divides into two or more daughter cells. _____ usually occurs as part of a larger cell cycle.

12. Reproduction

In eukaryotes, there are two distinct type of _____: a vegetative division, whereby each daughter cell is genetically identical to the parent cell (mitosis), and a reductive _____, whereby the number of chromosomes in the daughter cells is reduced by half, to produce haploid gametes (meiosis).

a. Smoothened
b. Shiga toxin
c. Cell division
d. Cystic fibrosis transmembrane conductance regulator

3. _____ is a hormone found in humans and other animals. It is synthesized and secreted by gonadotrophs of the anterior pituitary gland. Follicle stimulating hormone regulates the development, growth, pubertal maturation, and reproductive processes of the body.

a. Betatrophin
b. Big gastrin
c. Bovine somatotropin
d. Follicle-stimulating hormone

4. _____ is a special type of cell division necessary for sexual reproduction in eukaryotes, such as animals, plants and fungi. The number of sets of chromosomes in the cell undergoing _____ is reduced to half the original number, typically from two sets (diploid) to one set (haploid). The cells produced by _____ are either gametes (the usual case in animals) or otherwise usually spores from which gametes are ultimately produced (the case in land plants).

a. Bacterial one-hybrid system
b. Baek Sung-hee
c. Meiosis
d. BioScale Inc.

5. In molecular biology, _____ is a hormone produced by the syncytiotrophoblast, a component of the fertilized egg, after conception. Following implantation, the syncytiotrophoblast gives rise to the placenta. Some cancerous tumors produce this hormone; therefore, elevated levels measured when the patient is not pregnant can lead to a cancer diagnosis.

a. Human chorionic gonadotropin
b. Big gastrin
c. Bovine somatotropin
d. Bradykinin

1. c
2. c
3. d
4. c
5. a

You can take the complete Chapter Practice Test

for 12. Reproduction
on all key terms, persons, places, and concepts.

Online 99 Cents

http://www.JustTheFacts101.com

Use www.JustTheFacts101.com for all your study needs

including Facts101's online interactive problem solving labs in

chemistry, statistics, mathematics, and more.

_____ | Electrophoresis _____

_____ | Human genome _____

_____ | Antibody _____

CHAPTER HIGHLIGHTS & NOTES: KEY TERMS, PEOPLE, PLACES, CONCEPTS

Electrophoresis	Electrophoresis is the motion of dispersed particles relative to a fluid under the influence of a spatially uniform electric field. This electrokinetic phenomenon was observed for the first time in 1807 by Ferdinand Frederic Reuss (Moscow State University), who noticed that the application of a constant electric field caused clay particles dispersed in water to migrate. It is ultimately caused by the presence of a charged interface between the particle surface and the surrounding fluid.
Human genome	The human genome is the complete set of genetic information for humans . This information is located as DNA sequences within the 23 chromosome pairs in cell nuclei and in a small DNA molecule found within individual mitochondria. Human genomes include both protein-coding DNA genes and noncoding DNA. Haploid human genomes (contained in egg and sperm cells) consist of three billion DNA base pairs, while diploid genomes (found in somatic cells) have twice the DNA content.
Antibody	An antibody, also known as an immunoglobulin (Ig), is a large Y-shaped protein produced by B cells that is used by the immune system to identify and neutralize foreign objects such as bacteria and viruses. The antibody recognizes a unique part of the foreign target, called an antigen. Each tip of the 'Y' of an antibody contains a paratope (a structure analogous to a lock) that is specific for one particular epitope (similarly analogous to a key) on an antigen, allowing these two structures to bind together with precision.

13. Patterns of Inheritance

1. _____ is the motion of dispersed particles relative to a fluid under the influence of a spatially uniform electric field. This electrokinetic phenomenon was observed for the first time in 1807 by Ferdinand Frederic Reuss (Moscow State University), who noticed that the application of a constant electric field caused clay particles dispersed in water to migrate. It is ultimately caused by the presence of a charged interface between the particle surface and the surrounding fluid.

   a. 3-Hydroxyaspartic acid
   b. Chaconine
   c. Glycoalkaloid
   d. Electrophoresis

2. The _____ is the complete set of genetic information for humans . This information is located as DNA sequences within the 23 chromosome pairs in cell nuclei and in a small DNA molecule found within individual mitochondria. _____s include both protein-coding DNA genes and noncoding DNA. Haploid _____s (contained in egg and sperm cells) consist of three billion DNA base pairs, while diploid genomes (found in somatic cells) have twice the DNA content.

   a. Barley
   b. Bifidobacterium longum
   c. Bombyx mori
   d. Human genome

3. An _____, also known as an immunoglobulin (Ig), is a large Y-shaped protein produced by B cells that is used by the immune system to identify and neutralize foreign objects such as bacteria and viruses. The _____ recognizes a unique part of the foreign target, called an antigen. Each tip of the 'Y' of an _____ contains a paratope (a structure analogous to a lock) that is specific for one particular epitope (similarly analogous to a key) on an antigen, allowing these two structures to bind together with precision.

   a. 3-Hydroxyaspartic acid
   b. Antibody
   c. Glycoalkaloid
   d. Solamargine

1. d
2. d
3. b

You can take the complete Chapter Practice Test

for 13. Patterns of Inheritance
on all key terms, persons, places, and concepts.

Online 99 Cents

http://www.JustTheFacts101.com

Use www.JustTheFacts101.com for all your study needs

including Facts101's online interactive problem solving labs in

chemistry, statistics, mathematics, and more.

14. Other Forms of Inheritance

CHAPTER OUTLINE: KEY TERMS, PEOPLE, PLACES, CONCEPTS

	Intron
	Operon
	Response element
	Transcription factor
	Genomic imprinting
	X-inactivation
	Methylation
	Transposable element
	Retrotransposon

CHAPTER HIGHLIGHTS & NOTES: KEY TERMS, PEOPLE, PLACES, CONCEPTS

Intron	An intron is any nucleotide sequence within a gene that is removed by RNA splicing while the final mature RNA product of a gene is being generated. The term intron refers to both the DNA sequence within a gene and the corresponding sequence in RNA transcripts. Sequences that are joined together in the final mature RNA after RNA splicing are exons.
Operon	In genetics, an operon is a functioning unit of genomic DNA containing a cluster of genes under the control of a single regulatory signal or promoter. The genes are transcribed together into an mRNA strand and either translated together in the cytoplasm, or undergo trans-splicing to create monocistronic mRNAs that are translated separately, i.e. several strands of mRNA that each encode a single gene product. The result of this is that the genes contained in the operon are either expressed together or not at all.
Response element	Response elements are short sequences of DNA within a gene promoter region that are able to bind specific transcription factors and regulate transcription of genes. Under conditions of stress, a transcription activator protein binds to the response element and stimulates transcription.

14. Other Forms of Inheritance

Transcription factor	In molecular biology and genetics, a transcription factor is a protein that binds to specific DNA sequences, thereby controlling the flow (or transcription) of genetic information from DNA to messenger RNA. Transcription factors perform this function alone or with other proteins in a complex, by promoting (as an activator), or blocking (as a repressor) the recruitment of RNA polymerase (the enzyme that performs the transcription of genetic information from DNA to RNA) to specific genes. A defining feature of transcription factors is that they contain one or more DNA-binding domains (DBDs), which attach to specific sequences of DNA adjacent to the genes that they regulate. Additional proteins such as coactivators, chromatin remodelers, histone acetylases, deacetylases, kinases, and methylases, while also playing crucial roles in gene regulation, lack DNA-binding domains, and, therefore, are not classified as transcription factors.
Genomic imprinting	Genomic imprinting is an epigenetic phenomenon by which certain genes can be expressed in a parent-of-origin-specific manner. It may also ensure transposable elements remain epigenetically silenced throughout gametogenic reprogramming to maintain genome integrity. It is an inheritance process independent of the classical Mendelian inheritance.
X-inactivation	X-inactivation is a process by which one of the two copies of the X chromosome present in female mammals is inactivated. The inactive X chromosome is silenced by it being packaged in such a way that it has a transcriptionally inactive structure called heterochromatin. As female mammals have two X chromosomes, X-inactivation prevents them from having twice as many X chromosome gene products as males, which only possess a single copy of the X chromosome .
Methylation	In the chemical sciences, methylation denotes the addition of a methyl group to a substrate or the substitution of an atom or group by a methyl group. Methylation is a form of alkylation with a methyl group, rather than a larger carbon chain, replacing a hydrogen atom. These terms are commonly used in chemistry, biochemistry, soil science, and the biological sciences.
Transposable element	A transposable element is a DNA sequence that can change its position within the genome, sometimes creating or reversing mutations and altering the cell's genome size. Transposition often results in duplication of the TE. Barbara McClintock's discovery of these jumping genes earned her a Nobel prize in 1983. TEs make up a large fraction of the C-value of eukaryotic cells.
Retrotransposon	Retrotransposons are genetic elements that can amplify themselves in a genome and are ubiquitous components of the DNA of many eukaryotic organisms. They are a subclass of transposon. They are particularly abundant in plants, where they are often a principal component of nuclear DNA. In maize, 49-78% of the genome is made up of retrotransposons.

1. _____ is a process by which one of the two copies of the X chromosome present in female mammals is inactivated. The inactive X chromosome is silenced by it being packaged in such a way that it has a transcriptionally inactive structure called heterochromatin. As female mammals have two X chromosomes, _____ prevents them from having twice as many X chromosome gene products as males, which only possess a single copy of the X chromosome .

   a. Bacterial one-hybrid system
   b. Baek Sung-hee
   c. X-inactivation
   d. BioScale Inc.

2. An _____ is any nucleotide sequence within a gene that is removed by RNA splicing while the final mature RNA product of a gene is being generated. The term _____ refers to both the DNA sequence within a gene and the corresponding sequence in RNA transcripts. Sequences that are joined together in the final mature RNA after RNA splicing are exons.

   a. Intron
   b. CccDNA
   c. C-DNA
   d. Cell sorting

3. In the chemical sciences, _____ denotes the addition of a methyl group to a substrate or the substitution of an atom or group by a methyl group. _____ is a form of alkylation with a methyl group, rather than a larger carbon chain, replacing a hydrogen atom. These terms are commonly used in chemistry, biochemistry, soil science, and the biological sciences.

   a. Bile salt sulfotransferase
   b. Carboxylation
   c. Citrullination
   d. Methylation

4. _____ is an epigenetic phenomenon by which certain genes can be expressed in a parent-of-origin-specific manner. It may also ensure transposable elements remain epigenetically silenced throughout gametogenic reprogramming to maintain genome integrity. It is an inheritance process independent of the classical Mendelian inheritance.

   a. Bacterial transcription
   b. C1QL1
   c. CAG promoter
   d. Genomic imprinting

5. . In genetics, an _____ is a functioning unit of genomic DNA containing a cluster of genes under the control of a single regulatory signal or promoter. The genes are transcribed together into an mRNA strand and either translated together in the cytoplasm, or undergo trans-splicing to create monocistronic mRNAs that are translated separately, i.e. several strands of mRNA that each encode a single gene product. The result of this is that the genes contained in the _____ are either expressed together or not at all.

   a. Operon

b. C1QL1

c. CAG promoter

d. Capping enzyme

1. c
2. a
3. d
4. d
5. a

You can take the complete Chapter Practice Test

for 14. Other Forms of Inheritance
on all key terms, persons, places, and concepts.

Online 99 Cents

http://www.JustTheFacts101.com

Use www.JustTheFacts101.com for all your study needs

including Facts101's online interactive problem solving labs in

chemistry, statistics, mathematics, and more.

15. Advances in Molecular Genetics

CHAPTER OUTLINE: KEY TERMS, PEOPLE, PLACES, CONCEPTS

- Human genome
- Escherichia coli
- Genome project
- Caenorhabditis elegans
- Saccharomyces cerevisiae
- Functional genomics
- Cytochrome
- DNA repair
- Genetic engineering
- Growth hormone
- Microarray
- Restriction enzyme
- Plasmid
- DNA sequencing
- Polymerase chain reaction
- Taq polymerase
- Molecular genetics
- Point mutation
- Gene therapy
- Cystic fibrosis
- Hemoglobin

15. Advances in Molecular Genetics

Human genome	The human genome is the complete set of genetic information for humans . This information is located as DNA sequences within the 23 chromosome pairs in cell nuclei and in a small DNA molecule found within individual mitochondria. Human genomes include both protein-coding DNA genes and noncoding DNA. Haploid human genomes (contained in egg and sperm cells) consist of three billion DNA base pairs, while diploid genomes (found in somatic cells) have twice the DNA content.
Escherichia coli	Escherichia coli is a Gram-negative, facultative anaerobic, rod-shaped bacterium that is commonly found in the lower intestine of warm-blooded organisms (endotherms). Most E. coli strains are harmless, but some serotypes can cause serious food poisoning in humans, and are occasionally responsible for product recalls due to food contamination. The harmless strains are part of the normal flora of the gut, and can benefit their hosts by producing vitamin K_2, and by preventing the establishment of pathogenic bacteria within the intestine.
Genome project	Genome projects are scientific endeavours that ultimately aim to determine the complete genome sequence of an organism and to annotate protein-coding genes and other important genome-encoded features. The genome sequence of an organism includes the collective DNA sequences of each chromosome in the organism. For a bacterium containing a single chromosome, a genome project will aim to map the sequence of that chromosome.
Caenorhabditis elegans	Caenorhabditis elegans is a free-living, transparent nematode (roundworm), about 1 mm in length, that lives in temperate soil environments. The name is a blend of Greek (caeno- - recent, rhabditis - rod-like) and Latin (elegans - elegant). In 1900, Maupas initially named it Rhabditides elegans, Osche placed it in the subgenus Caenorhabditis in 1952, and Dougherty raised it to generic status in 1955. In 1974, Sydney Brenner began research into the molecular and developmental biology of C. elegans, which has since been extensively used as a model organism.
Saccharomyces cerevisiae	Saccharomyces cerevisiae is a species of yeast. It is perhaps the most useful yeast, having been instrumental to winemaking, baking and brewing since ancient times. It is believed that it was originally isolated from the skin of grapes .
Functional genomics	Functional genomics is a field of molecular biology that attempts to make use of the vast wealth of data produced by genomic projects to describe gene (and protein) functions and interactions. Unlike genomics, functional genomics focuses on the dynamic aspects such as gene transcription, translation, and protein-protein interactions, as opposed to the static aspects of the genomic information such as DNA sequence or structures. Functional genomics attempts to answer questions about the function of DNA at the levels of genes, RNA transcripts, and protein products.
Cytochrome	Cytochromes are, in general, membrane-bound hemeproteins containing heme groups and are primarily responsible for the generation of ATP via electron transport.

DNA repair	DNA repair is a collection of processes by which a cell identifies and corrects damage to the DNA molecules that encode its genome. In human cells, both normal metabolic activities and environmental factors such as UV light and radiation can cause DNA damage, resulting in as many as 1 million individual molecular lesions per cell per day. Many of these lesions cause structural damage to the DNA molecule and can alter or eliminate the cell's ability to transcribe the gene that the affected DNA encodes.
Genetic engineering	Genetic engineering, also called genetic modification, is the direct manipulation of an organism's genome using biotechnology. New DNA may be inserted in the host genome by first isolating and copying the genetic material of interest using molecular cloning methods to generate a DNA sequence, or by synthesizing the DNA, and then inserting this construct into the host organism. Genes may be removed, or 'knocked out', using a nuclease.
Growth hormone	Growth hormone, also known as somatotropin or somatropin, is a peptide hormone that stimulates growth, cell reproduction and regeneration in humans and other animals. It is a type of mitogen which is specific only to certain kinds of cells. Growth hormone is a 191-amino acid, single-chain polypeptide that is synthesized, stored, and secreted by somatotropic cells within the lateral wings of the anterior pituitary gland.
Microarray	A microarray is a multiplex lab-on-a-chip. It is a 2D array on a solid substrate (usually a glass slide or silicon thin-film cell) that assays large amounts of biological material using high-throughput screening methods. The concept and methodology of microarrays was first introduced and illustrated in antibody microarrays (also referred to as antibody matrix) in 1983 in a scientific publication and a series of patents.
Restriction enzyme	A restriction enzyme is an enzyme that cuts DNA at or near specific recognition nucleotide sequences known as restriction sites. Restriction enzymes are commonly classified into three types, which differ in their structure and whether they cut their DNA substrate at their recognition site, or if the recognition and cleavage sites are separate from one another. To cut DNA, all restriction enzymes make two incisions, once through each sugar-phosphate backbone (i.e. each strand) of the DNA double helix.
Plasmid	A plasmid is a small DNA molecule that is physically separate from, and can replicate independently of, chromosomal DNA within a cell. Most commonly found as small circular, double-stranded DNA molecules in bacteria, plasmids are sometimes present in archaea and eukaryotic organisms. In nature, plasmids carry genes that may benefit survival of the organism (e.g. antibiotic resistance), and can frequently be transmitted from one bacterium to another (even of another species) via horizontal gene transfer.
DNA sequencing	DNA sequencing is the process of determining the precise order of nucleotides within a DNA molecule. It includes any method or technology that is used to determine the order of the four bases--adenine, guanine, cytosine, and thymine--in a strand of DNA.

15. Advances in Molecular Genetics

The advent of rapid DNA sequencing methods has greatly accelerated biological and medical research and discovery.

Knowledge of DNA sequences has become indispensable for basic biological research, and in numerous applied fields such as diagnostic, biotechnology, forensic biology, and biological systematics.

Polymerase chain reaction

The polymerase chain reaction is a biochemical technology in molecular biology to amplify a single or a few copies of a piece of DNA across several orders of magnitude, generating thousands to millions of copies of a particular DNA sequence.

Developed in 1983 by Kary Mullis, Polymerase chain reaction is now a common and often indispensable technique used in medical and biological research labs for a variety of applications. These include DNA cloning for sequencing, DNA-based phylogeny, or functional analysis of genes; the diagnosis of hereditary diseases; the identification of genetic fingerprints (used in forensic sciences and paternity testing); and the detection and diagnosis of infectious diseases.

Taq polymerase

Taq polymerase is a thermostable DNA polymerase named after the thermophilic bacterium Thermus aquaticus from which it was originally isolated by Thomas D. Brock in 1965. It is often abbreviated to 'Taq Pol' (or simply 'Taq'), and is frequently used in polymerase chain reaction (PCR), a method for greatly amplifying short segments of DNA.

T. aquaticus is a bacterium that lives in hot springs and hydrothermal vents, and Taq polymerase was identified as an enzyme able to withstand the protein-denaturing conditions (high temperature) required during PCR. Therefore it replaced the DNA polymerase from E. coli originally used in PCR. Taq's optimum temperature for activity is 75-80°C, with a half-life of greater than 2 hours at 92.5°C, 40 minutes at 95°C and 9 minutes at 97.5°C, and can replicate a 1000 base pair strand of DNA in less than 10 seconds at 72°C.

One of Taq's drawbacks is its relatively low replication fidelity. It lacks a 3' to 5' exonuclease proofreading activity, and has an error rate measured at about 1 in 9,000 nucleotides. The remaining two domains however may act in coordination, via coupled domain motion.

Molecular genetics

Molecular genetics is the field of biology and genetics that studies the structure and function of genes at a molecular level. Molecular genetics employs the methods of genetics and molecular biology to elucidate molecular function and interactions among genes. It is so called to differentiate it from other sub fields of genetics such as ecological genetics and population genetics.

Point mutation

A point mutation, or single base substitution, is a type of mutation that causes the replacement of a single base nucleotide with another nucleotide of the genetic material, DNA or RNA. The term point mutation also includes insertions or deletions of a single base pair.

A point mutant is an individual that is affected by a point mutation.

Repeat induced point mutations are recurring point mutations, discussed below.

Gene therapy	Gene therapy is the use of DNA as a pharmaceutical agent to treat disease. It derives its name from the idea that DNA can be used to supplement or alter genes within an individual's cells as a therapy to treat disease. The most common form of gene therapy involves using DNA that encodes a functional, therapeutic gene to replace a mutated gene.
Cystic fibrosis	Cystic fibrosis, also known as mucoviscidosis, is an autosomal recessive genetic disorder that affects most critically the lungs, and also the pancreas, liver, and intestine. It is characterized by abnormal transport of chloride and sodium across an epithelium, leading to thick, viscous secretions.
	The name cystic fibrosis refers to the characteristic scarring (fibrosis) and cyst formation within the pancreas, first recognized in the 1930s.
Hemoglobin	Haemoglobin ; also spelled hemoglobin and abbreviated Hb or Hgb, is the iron-containing oxygen-transport metalloprotein in the red blood cells of all vertebrates as well as the tissues of some invertebrates. Hemoglobin in the blood carries oxygen from the respiratory organs (lungs or gills) to the rest of the body (i.e. the tissues) where it releases the oxygen to burn nutrients to provide energy to power the functions of the organism, and collects the resultant carbon dioxide to bring it back to the respiratory organs to be dispensed from the organism.
	In mammals, the protein makes up about 97% of the red blood cells' dry content (by weight), and around 35% of the total content (including water).

15. Advances in Molecular Genetics

1. _____, also known as mucoviscidosis, is an autosomal recessive genetic disorder that affects most critically the lungs, and also the pancreas, liver, and intestine. It is characterized by abnormal transport of chloride and sodium across an epithelium, leading to thick, viscous secretions.

   The name _____ refers to the characteristic scarring (fibrosis) and cyst formation within the pancreas, first recognized in the 1930s.

   a. Bartter syndrome
   b. Benign familial neonatal epilepsy
   c. Brugada syndrome
   d. Cystic fibrosis

2. _____, also called genetic modification, is the direct manipulation of an organism's genome using biotechnology. New DNA may be inserted in the host genome by first isolating and copying the genetic material of interest using molecular cloning methods to generate a DNA sequence, or by synthesizing the DNA, and then inserting this construct into the host organism. Genes may be removed, or 'knocked out', using a nuclease.

   a. Bacterial artificial chromosome
   b. Bacterial conjugation
   c. Genetic engineering
   d. Base calling

3. _____ is a collection of processes by which a cell identifies and corrects damage to the DNA molecules that encode its genome. In human cells, both normal metabolic activities and environmental factors such as UV light and radiation can cause DNA damage, resulting in as many as 1 million individual molecular lesions per cell per day. Many of these lesions cause structural damage to the DNA molecule and can alter or eliminate the cell's ability to transcribe the gene that the affected DNA encodes.

   a. DNA repair
   b. Chaconine
   c. Glycoalkaloid
   d. Solamargine

4. . _____ is a Gram-negative, facultative anaerobic, rod-shaped bacterium that is commonly found in the lower intestine of warm-blooded organisms (endotherms). Most E. coli strains are harmless, but some serotypes can cause serious food poisoning in humans, and are occasionally responsible for product recalls due to food contamination. The harmless strains are part of the normal flora of the gut, and can benefit their hosts by producing vitamin K_2, and by preventing the establishment of pathogenic bacteria within the intestine.

   a. Barley
   b. Bifidobacterium longum
   c. Escherichia coli

5. A _____ is a small DNA molecule that is physically separate from, and can replicate independently of, chromosomal DNA within a cell. Most commonly found as small circular, double-stranded DNA molecules in bacteria, _____s are sometimes present in archaea and eukaryotic organisms. In nature, _____s carry genes that may benefit survival of the organism (e.g. antibiotic resistance), and can frequently be transmitted from one bacterium to another (even of another species) via horizontal gene transfer.

   a. Plasmid
   b. Bacterial conjugation
   c. BamHI
   d. Base calling

1. d
2. c
3. a
4. c
5. a

You can take the complete Chapter Practice Test

for 15. Advances in Molecular Genetics
on all key terms, persons, places, and concepts.

Online 99 Cents

http://www.JustTheFacts101.com

Use www.JustTheFacts101.com for all your study needs

including Facts101's online interactive problem solving labs in

chemistry, statistics, mathematics, and more.

CHAPTER OUTLINE: KEY TERMS, PEOPLE, PLACES, CONCEPTS

	DNA repair
	Hemoglobin
	DNA polymerase
	Genome project
	Human genome

CHAPTER HIGHLIGHTS & NOTES: KEY TERMS, PEOPLE, PLACES, CONCEPTS

DNA repair	DNA repair is a collection of processes by which a cell identifies and corrects damage to the DNA molecules that encode its genome. In human cells, both normal metabolic activities and environmental factors such as UV light and radiation can cause DNA damage, resulting in as many as 1 million individual molecular lesions per cell per day. Many of these lesions cause structural damage to the DNA molecule and can alter or eliminate the cell's ability to transcribe the gene that the affected DNA encodes.
Hemoglobin	Haemoglobin ; also spelled hemoglobin and abbreviated Hb or Hgb, is the iron-containing oxygen-transport metalloprotein in the red blood cells of all vertebrates as well as the tissues of some invertebrates. Hemoglobin in the blood carries oxygen from the respiratory organs (lungs or gills) to the rest of the body (i.e. the tissues) where it releases the oxygen to burn nutrients to provide energy to power the functions of the organism, and collects the resultant carbon dioxide to bring it back to the respiratory organs to be dispensed from the organism. In mammals, the protein makes up about 97% of the red blood cells' dry content (by weight), and around 35% of the total content (including water).
DNA polymerase	A DNA polymerase is a cellular or viral polymerase enzyme that synthesizes DNA molecules from their nucleotide building blocks. DNA polymerases are essential for DNA replication, and usually function in pairs while copying one double-stranded DNA molecule into two double-stranded DNAs in a process termed semiconservative DNA replication. DNA polymerases also play key roles in other processes within cells, including DNA repair, genetic recombination, reverse transcription, and the generation of antibody diversity via the specialized DNA polymerase, terminal deoxynucleotidyl transferase.

16. Population Genetics

Genome project	Genome projects are scientific endeavours that ultimately aim to determine the complete genome sequence of an organism and to annotate protein-coding genes and other important genome-encoded features. The genome sequence of an organism includes the collective DNA sequences of each chromosome in the organism. For a bacterium containing a single chromosome, a genome project will aim to map the sequence of that chromosome.
Human genome	The human genome is the complete set of genetic information for humans . This information is located as DNA sequences within the 23 chromosome pairs in cell nuclei and in a small DNA molecule found within individual mitochondria. Human genomes include both protein-coding DNA genes and noncoding DNA. Haploid human genomes (contained in egg and sperm cells) consist of three billion DNA base pairs, while diploid genomes (found in somatic cells) have twice the DNA content.

1. A _____ is a cellular or viral polymerase enzyme that synthesizes DNA molecules from their nucleotide building blocks. _____s are essential for DNA replication, and usually function in pairs while copying one double-stranded DNA molecule into two double-stranded DNAs in a process termed semiconservative DNA replication. _____s also play key roles in other processes within cells, including DNA repair, genetic recombination, reverse transcription, and the generation of antibody diversity via the specialized _____, terminal deoxynucleotidyl transferase.

   a. Binding site
   b. CccDNA
   c. C-DNA
   d. DNA polymerase

2. _____ is a collection of processes by which a cell identifies and corrects damage to the DNA molecules that encode its genome. In human cells, both normal metabolic activities and environmental factors such as UV light and radiation can cause DNA damage, resulting in as many as 1 million individual molecular lesions per cell per day. Many of these lesions cause structural damage to the DNA molecule and can alter or eliminate the cell's ability to transcribe the gene that the affected DNA encodes.

   a. 3-Hydroxyaspartic acid
   b. Chaconine
   c. Glycoalkaloid
   d. DNA repair

3. . Haemoglobin ; also spelled _____ and abbreviated Hb or Hgb, is the iron-containing oxygen-transport metalloprotein in the red blood cells of all vertebrates as well as the tissues of some invertebrates.

_____ in the blood carries oxygen from the respiratory organs (lungs or gills) to the rest of the body (i.e. the tissues) where it releases the oxygen to burn nutrients to provide energy to power the functions of the organism, and collects the resultant carbon dioxide to bring it back to the respiratory organs to be dispensed from the organism.

In mammals, the protein makes up about 97% of the red blood cells' dry content (by weight), and around 35% of the total content (including water).

a. Hemoglobin
b. Fetal hemoglobin
c. Glycated hemoglobin
d. Hb Bassett

4. _____s are scientific endeavours that ultimately aim to determine the complete genome sequence of an organism and to annotate protein-coding genes and other important genome-encoded features. The genome sequence of an organism includes the collective DNA sequences of each chromosome in the organism. For a bacterium containing a single chromosome, a _____ will aim to map the sequence of that chromosome.

a. 100K Genome Project
b. Genome project
c. Shiga toxin
d. Shiga-like toxin

5. The _____ is the complete set of genetic information for humans . This information is located as DNA sequences within the 23 chromosome pairs in cell nuclei and in a small DNA molecule found within individual mitochondria.
    _____s include both protein-coding DNA genes and noncoding DNA. Haploid _____s (contained in egg and sperm cells) consist of three billion DNA base pairs, while diploid genomes (found in somatic cells) have twice the DNA content.

a. Human genome
b. Bifidobacterium longum
c. Bombyx mori
d. Botryllus schlosseri

1. d
2. d
3. a
4. b
5. a

You can take the complete Chapter Practice Test

for 16. Population Genetics
on all key terms, persons, places, and concepts.

Online 99 Cents

http://www.JustTheFacts101.com

Use www.JustTheFacts101.com for all your study needs

including Facts101's online interactive problem solving labs in

chemistry, statistics, mathematics, and more.

17. The Origin of Life

CHAPTER OUTLINE: KEY TERMS, PEOPLE, PLACES, CONCEPTS

	Amino acid
	DNA replication
	Ribozyme

CHAPTER HIGHLIGHTS & NOTES: KEY TERMS, PEOPLE, PLACES, CONCEPTS

Amino acid — Amino acids are biologically important organic compounds made from amine ($-NH_2$) and carboxylic acid ($-COOH$) functional groups, along with a side-chain specific to each amino acid. The key elements of an amino acid are carbon, hydrogen, oxygen, and nitrogen, though other elements are found in the side-chains of certain amino acids. About 500 amino acids are known and can be classified in many ways.

DNA replication — DNA replication is the process of producing two identical copies from one original DNA molecule. This biological process occurs in all living organisms and is the basis for biological inheritance. DNA is composed of two strands and each strand of the original DNA molecule serves as template for the production of the complementary strand, a process referred to as semiconservative replication.

Ribozyme — A ribozyme is an RNA molecule that is capable of performing specific biochemical reactions, similar to the action of protein enzymes. The 1981 discovery of ribozymes demonstrated that RNA can be both genetic material (like DNA) and a biological catalyst (like protein enzymes), and contributed to the RNA world hypothesis, which suggests that RNA may have been important in the evolution of prebiotic self-replicating systems. Also termed catalytic RNA, ribozymes function within the ribosome (as part of the large subunit ribosomal RNA) to link amino acids during protein synthesis, and in a variety of RNA processing reactions, including RNA splicing, viral replication, and transfer RNA biosynthesis.

Visit Cram101.com for full Practice Exams

1. A _____ is an RNA molecule that is capable of performing specific biochemical reactions, similar to the action of protein enzymes. The 1981 discovery of _____s demonstrated that RNA can be both genetic material (like DNA) and a biological catalyst (like protein enzymes), and contributed to the RNA world hypothesis, which suggests that RNA may have been important in the evolution of prebiotic self-replicating systems. Also termed catalytic RNA, _____s function within the ribosome (as part of the large subunit ribosomal RNA) to link amino acids during protein synthesis, and in a variety of RNA processing reactions, including RNA splicing, viral replication, and transfer RNA biosynthesis.

   a. Ribozyme
   b. 3-Monoacetylmorphine
   c. -4-Hydroxy-3-methyl-but-2-enyl pyrophosphate
   d. 5-Bromouracil

2. _____s are biologically important organic compounds made from amine (-NH$_2$) and carboxylic acid (-COOH) functional groups, along with a side-chain specific to each _____. The key elements of an _____ are carbon, hydrogen, oxygen, and nitrogen, though other elements are found in the side-chains of certain _____s. About 500 _____s are known and can be classified in many ways.

   a. Chaconine
   b. Amino acid
   c. Solamargine
   d. Solanine

3. _____ is the process of producing two identical copies from one original DNA molecule. This biological process occurs in all living organisms and is the basis for biological inheritance. DNA is composed of two strands and each strand of the original DNA molecule serves as template for the production of the complementary strand, a process referred to as semiconservative replication.

   a. 3-Hydroxyaspartic acid
   b. DNA replication
   c. Glycoalkaloid
   d. Solamargine

1. a
2. b
3. b

You can take the complete Chapter Practice Test

for 17. The Origin of Life
on all key terms, persons, places, and concepts.

Online 99 Cents

http://www.JustTheFacts101.com

Use www.JustTheFacts101.com for all your study needs

including Facts101's online interactive problem solving labs in

chemistry, statistics, mathematics, and more.

18. Diversity and Variation

	Giant panda
	Molecular clock
	Chitin

CHAPTER HIGHLIGHTS & NOTES: KEY TERMS, PEOPLE, PLACES, CONCEPTS

Giant panda	The panda, also known as the giant panda to distinguish it from the unrelated red panda, is a bear native to south central China. It is easily recognized by the large, distinctive black patches around its eyes, over the ears, and across its round body. Though it belongs to the order Carnivora, the panda's diet is 99% bamboo.
Molecular clock	The molecular clock is a technique in molecular evolution that uses fossil constraints and rates of molecular change to deduce the time in geologic history when two species or other taxa diverged. It is used to estimate the time of occurrence of events called speciation or radiation. The molecular data used for such calculations is usually nucleotide sequences for DNA or amino acid sequences for proteins.
Chitin	Chitin $_n$ (-tin) is a long-chain polymer of a N-acetylglucosamine, a derivative of glucose, and is found in many places throughout the natural world. It is the main component of the cell walls of fungi, the exoskeletons of arthropods such as crustaceans (e.g., crabs, lobsters and shrimps) and insects, the radulas of mollusks, and the beaks and internal shells of cephalopods, including squid and octopuses. In terms of structure, chitin may be compared to the polysaccharide cellulose and, exist in nature in the form of nanocrystallites named nanofibrils or whiskers .

1. _____ n (-tin) is a long-chain polymer of a N-acetylglucosamine, a derivative of glucose, and is found in many places throughout the natural world. It is the main component of the cell walls of fungi, the exoskeletons of arthropods such as crustaceans (e.g., crabs, lobsters and shrimps) and insects, the radulas of mollusks, and the beaks and internal shells of cephalopods, including squid and octopuses. In terms of structure, _____ may be compared to the polysaccharide cellulose and, exist in nature in the form of nanocrystallites named nanofibrils or whiskers .

    a. 1,3-Bisphosphoglyceric acid
    b. 5-Bromouracil
    c. Chitin
    d. Bacillibactin

2. The panda, also known as the _____ to distinguish it from the unrelated red panda, is a bear native to south central China. It is easily recognized by the large, distinctive black patches around its eyes, over the ears, and across its round body. Though it belongs to the order Carnivora, the panda's diet is 99% bamboo.

    a. Barley
    b. Bifidobacterium longum
    c. Bombyx mori
    d. Giant panda

3. The _____ is a technique in molecular evolution that uses fossil constraints and rates of molecular change to deduce the time in geologic history when two species or other taxa diverged. It is used to estimate the time of occurrence of events called speciation or radiation. The molecular data used for such calculations is usually nucleotide sequences for DNA or amino acid sequences for proteins.

    a. Chimeric gene
    b. Gene conversion
    c. Molecular clock
    d. Genome evolution

1. c
2. d
3. c

You can take the complete Chapter Practice Test

for 18. Diversity and Variation
on all key terms, persons, places, and concepts.

Online 99 Cents

http://www.JustTheFacts101.com

Use www.JustTheFacts101.com for all your study needs

including Facts101's online interactive problem solving labs in

chemistry, statistics, mathematics, and more.

19. Changes in Species

CHAPTER OUTLINE: KEY TERMS, PEOPLE, PLACES, CONCEPTS

	DNA repair
	Genetic code
	Hox gene
	Molecular genetics

CHAPTER HIGHLIGHTS & NOTES: KEY TERMS, PEOPLE, PLACES, CONCEPTS

DNA repair	DNA repair is a collection of processes by which a cell identifies and corrects damage to the DNA molecules that encode its genome. In human cells, both normal metabolic activities and environmental factors such as UV light and radiation can cause DNA damage, resulting in as many as 1 million individual molecular lesions per cell per day. Many of these lesions cause structural damage to the DNA molecule and can alter or eliminate the cell's ability to transcribe the gene that the affected DNA encodes.
Genetic code	The genetic code is the set of rules by which information encoded within genetic material is translated into proteins by living cells. Biological decoding is accomplished by the ribosome, which links amino acids in an order specified by mRNA, using transfer RNA (tRNA) molecules to carry amino acids and to read the mRNA three nucleotides at a time. The genetic code is highly similar among all organisms and can be expressed in a simple table with 64 entries.
Hox gene	Hox genes are a group of related genes that control the body plan of the embryo along the anterior-posterior (head-tail) axis. After the embryonic segments have formed, the Hox proteins determine the type of segment structures (e.g. legs, antennae, and wings in fruit flies or the different vertebrate ribs in humans) that will form on a given segment. Hox proteins thus confer segmental identity, but do not form the actual segments themselves

Hox genes are defined as having the following properties:•their protein product is a transcription factor•they contain a DNA sequence known as the homeobox•in many animals, the organization of the Hox genes on the chromosome is the same as the order of their expression along the anterior-posterior axis of the developing animal, and are thus said to display colinearity.. |
| Molecular genetics | Molecular genetics is the field of biology and genetics that studies the structure and function of genes at a molecular level. Molecular genetics employs the methods of genetics and molecular biology to elucidate molecular function and interactions among genes. |

Visit Cram101.com for full Practice Exams

1. The _____ is the set of rules by which information encoded within genetic material is translated into proteins by living cells. Biological decoding is accomplished by the ribosome, which links amino acids in an order specified by mRNA, using transfer RNA (tRNA) molecules to carry amino acids and to read the mRNA three nucleotides at a time. The _____ is highly similar among all organisms and can be expressed in a simple table with 64 entries.

 a. Bacterial transcription
 b. C1QL1
 c. CAG promoter
 d. Genetic code

2. _____ is a collection of processes by which a cell identifies and corrects damage to the DNA molecules that encode its genome. In human cells, both normal metabolic activities and environmental factors such as UV light and radiation can cause DNA damage, resulting in as many as 1 million individual molecular lesions per cell per day. Many of these lesions cause structural damage to the DNA molecule and can alter or eliminate the cell's ability to transcribe the gene that the affected DNA encodes.

 a. DNA repair
 b. Chaconine
 c. Glycoalkaloid
 d. Solamargine

3. _____s are a group of related genes that control the body plan of the embryo along the anterior-posterior (head-tail) axis. After the embryonic segments have formed, the Hox proteins determine the type of segment structures (e.g. legs, antennae, and wings in fruit flies or the different vertebrate ribs in humans) that will form on a given segment. Hox proteins thus confer segmental identity, but do not form the actual segments themselves

 _____s are defined as having the following properties:•their protein product is a transcription factor•they contain a DNA sequence known as the homeobox•in many animals, the organization of the _____s on the chromosome is the same as the order of their expression along the anterior-posterior axis of the developing animal, and are thus said to display colinearity..

 a. BMPR2
 b. Bone morphogenetic protein 1
 c. Bone morphogenetic protein 10
 d. Hox gene

4. . _____ is the field of biology and genetics that studies the structure and function of genes at a molecular level. _____ employs the methods of genetics and molecular biology to elucidate molecular function and interactions among genes. It is so called to differentiate it from other sub fields of genetics such as ecological genetics and population genetics.

 a. Molecular genetics
 b. Bacterial conjugation
 c. BamHI

1. d
2. a
3. d
4. a

You can take the complete Chapter Practice Test

for 19. Changes in Species
on all key terms, persons, places, and concepts.

Online 99 Cents

http://www.JustTheFacts101.com

Use www.JustTheFacts101.com for all your study needs

including Facts101's online interactive problem solving labs in

chemistry, statistics, mathematics, and more.

CHAPTER OUTLINE: KEY TERMS, PEOPLE, PLACES, CONCEPTS

	Antibody
	Molecular genetics
	Escherichia coli
	Frequency

CHAPTER HIGHLIGHTS & NOTES: KEY TERMS, PEOPLE, PLACES, CONCEPTS

Antibody	An antibody, also known as an immunoglobulin (Ig), is a large Y-shaped protein produced by B cells that is used by the immune system to identify and neutralize foreign objects such as bacteria and viruses. The antibody recognizes a unique part of the foreign target, called an antigen. Each tip of the 'Y' of an antibody contains a paratope (a structure analogous to a lock) that is specific for one particular epitope (similarly analogous to a key) on an antigen, allowing these two structures to bind together with precision.
Molecular genetics	Molecular genetics is the field of biology and genetics that studies the structure and function of genes at a molecular level. Molecular genetics employs the methods of genetics and molecular biology to elucidate molecular function and interactions among genes. It is so called to differentiate it from other sub fields of genetics such as ecological genetics and population genetics.
Escherichia coli	Escherichia coli is a Gram-negative, facultative anaerobic, rod-shaped bacterium that is commonly found in the lower intestine of warm-blooded organisms (endotherms). Most E. coli strains are harmless, but some serotypes can cause serious food poisoning in humans, and are occasionally responsible for product recalls due to food contamination. The harmless strains are part of the normal flora of the gut, and can benefit their hosts by producing vitamin K_2, and by preventing the establishment of pathogenic bacteria within the intestine.
Frequency	Frequency is a gene discovered in the fungus Neurospora crassa in 1978 that encodes the protein frequency. The gene is 2,980bp long in Sordaria macrospora k-hell. The FRQ protein plays a key role in the autoregulatory transcription translation negative feedback loop (TTFL), which is responsible for circadian rhythms in N. crassa and other fungi such as N. sitophita, N. tetrasperma, N. galapagosensis, C. spinulosa, and L. australiensis.

20. Human Evolution

1. An _____, also known as an immunoglobulin (Ig), is a large Y-shaped protein produced by B cells that is used by the immune system to identify and neutralize foreign objects such as bacteria and viruses. The _____ recognizes a unique part of the foreign target, called an antigen. Each tip of the 'Y' of an _____ contains a paratope (a structure analogous to a lock) that is specific for one particular epitope (similarly analogous to a key) on an antigen, allowing these two structures to bind together with precision.

   a. 3-Hydroxyaspartic acid
   b. Antibody
   c. Glycoalkaloid
   d. Solamargine

2. _____ is the field of biology and genetics that studies the structure and function of genes at a molecular level. _____ employs the methods of genetics and molecular biology to elucidate molecular function and interactions among genes. It is so called to differentiate it from other sub fields of genetics such as ecological genetics and population genetics.

   a. Molecular genetics
   b. Bacterial conjugation
   c. BamHI
   d. Base calling

3. _____ is a Gram-negative, facultative anaerobic, rod-shaped bacterium that is commonly found in the lower intestine of warm-blooded organisms (endotherms). Most E. coli strains are harmless, but some serotypes can cause serious food poisoning in humans, and are occasionally responsible for product recalls due to food contamination. The harmless strains are part of the normal flora of the gut, and can benefit their hosts by producing vitamin K_2, and by preventing the establishment of pathogenic bacteria within the intestine.

   a. Escherichia coli
   b. Bifidobacterium longum
   c. Bombyx mori
   d. Botryllus schlosseri

4. _____ is a gene discovered in the fungus Neurospora crassa in 1978 that encodes the protein _____. The gene is 2,980bp long in Sordaria macrospora k-hell. The FRQ protein plays a key role in the autoregulatory transcription translation negative feedback loop (TTFL), which is responsible for circadian rhythms in N. crassa and other fungi such as N. sitophita, N. tetrasperma, N. galapagosensis, C. spinulosa, and L. australiensis.

   a. 14-3-3 protein
   b. Frequency
   c. Barnase
   d. Bcl-2-associated death promoter

1. b
2. a
3. a
4. b

You can take the complete Chapter Practice Test

for 20. Human Evolution
on all key terms, persons, places, and concepts.

Online 99 Cents

http://www.JustTheFacts101.com

Use www.JustTheFacts101.com for all your study needs

including Facts101's online interactive problem solving labs in

chemistry, statistics, mathematics, and more.

	Sensory receptor
	Receptor
	Effector
	Action potential
	Neurotransmitter
	Amino acid
	Dopamine
	Nitric oxide
	Peptide
	Amphetamine
	Caffeine
	Cocaine
	Nicotine
	Mescaline
	Molecular biology
	Molecular evolution
	Tetrodotoxin

21. Nervous Systems

Sensory receptor	In a sensory system, a sensory receptor is a sensory nerve ending that responds to a stimulus in the internal or external environment of an organism. In response to stimuli, the sensory receptor initiates sensory transduction by creating graded potentials or action potentials in the same cell or in an adjacent one.
Receptor	In the field of biochemistry, a receptor is a molecule usually found on the surface of a cell, that receives chemical signals from outside the cell. When such external substances bind to a receptor, they direct the cell to do something, such as divide, die, or allow specific substances to enter or exit the cell.
	Receptors are proteins embedded in either the cell's plasma membrane (cell surface receptors), in the cytoplasm, or in the cell's nucleus (nuclear receptors), to which specific signaling molecules may attach.
Effector	In biochemistry, an effector molecule is usually a small molecule that selectively binds to a protein and regulates its biological activity. In this manner, effector molecules act as ligands that can increase or decrease enzyme activity, gene expression, or cell signalling. Effector molecules can also directly regulate the activity of some mRNA molecules (riboswitches).
Action potential	In physiology, an action potential is a short-lasting event in which the electrical membrane potential of a cell rapidly rises and falls, following a consistent trajectory. Action potentials occur in several types of animal cells, called excitable cells, which include neurons, muscle cells, and endocrine cells, as well as in some plant cells. In neurons, they play a central role in cell-to-cell communication.
Neurotransmitter	Neurotransmitters are endogenous chemicals that transmit signals from a neuron to a target cell across a synapse. Neurotransmitters are packaged into synaptic vesicles clustered beneath the membrane in the axon terminal, on the presynaptic side of a synapse. They are released into and diffuse across the synaptic cleft, where they bind to specific receptors in the membrane on the postsynaptic side of the synapse.
Amino acid	Amino acids are biologically important organic compounds made from amine ($-NH_2$) and carboxylic acid ($-COOH$) functional groups, along with a side-chain specific to each amino acid. The key elements of an amino acid are carbon, hydrogen, oxygen, and nitrogen, though other elements are found in the side-chains of certain amino acids. About 500 amino acids are known and can be classified in many ways.
Dopamine	Dopamine is a simple organic chemical in the catecholamine and phenethylamine families that plays a number of important roles in the brains and bodies of animals. Its name derives from its chemical structure: it is an amine that is formed by removing a carboxyl group from a molecule of L-DOPA.

In the brain, dopamine functions as a neurotransmitter--a chemical released by nerve cells to send signals to other nerve cells. The brain includes several distinct dopamine systems, one of which plays a major role in reward-motivated behavior.

Nitric oxide	Nitric oxide, or nitrogen oxide, also known as nitrogen monoxide, is a molecule with chemical formula NO. It is a free radical and is an important intermediate in the chemical industry. Nitric oxide is a by-product of combustion of substances in the air, as in automobile engines, fossil fuel power plants, and is produced naturally during the electrical discharges of lightning in thunderstorms. In mammals including humans, NO is an important cellular signaling molecule involved in many physiological and pathological processes.
Peptide	Peptides are short chains of amino acid monomers linked by peptide bonds. The covalent chemical bonds are formed when the carboxyl group of one amino acid reacts with the amino group of another. The shortest peptides are dipeptides, consisting of 2 amino acids joined by a single peptide bond, followed by tripeptides, tetrapeptides, etc.
Amphetamine	Amphetamine is a potent central nervous system (CNS) stimulant of the phenethylamine class that is used to treat attention deficit hyperactivity disorder (ADHD) and narcolepsy. Historically, it has been used medically as a nasal decongestant and as a treatment for depression and obesity. Amphetamine is also used as a performance and cognitive enhancer, and, in spite of the significant health risks associated with uncontrolled or high dose use, some individuals use it recreationally as an aphrodisiac or a euphoriant.
Caffeine	Caffeine is a bitter, white crystalline xanthine alkaloid and a stimulant drug. Caffeine is found in varying quantities in the seeds, leaves, and fruit of some plants, where it acts as a natural pesticide that paralyzes and kills certain insects feeding on the plants, as well as enhancing the reward memory of pollinators. It is most commonly consumed by humans in infusions extracted from the seed of the coffee plant and the leaves of the tea bush, as well as from various foods and drinks containing products derived from the kola nut.
Cocaine	Cocaine is a crystalline tropane alkaloid that is obtained from the leaves of the coca plant. The name comes from 'coca' and the alkaloid suffix '-ine', forming 'cocaine'. It is a stimulant, an appetite suppressant, and a nonspecific voltage gated sodium channel blocker, which in turn causes it to produce anaesthesia at low doses.
Nicotine	Nicotine is a potent parasympathomimetic alkaloid found in the nightshade family of plants and a stimulant drug. It is a nicotinic acetylcholine receptor agonist. It is made in the roots and accumulates in the leaves of the plants.

21. Nervous Systems

Mescaline	Mescaline or 3,4,5-trimethoxyphenethylamine is a naturally occurring psychedelic alkaloid of the phenethylamine class, known for its mind-altering effects similar to those of LSD and psilocybin. It occurs naturally in the peyote cactus, the San Pedro cactus (Echinopsis pachanoi) and in the Peruvian torch (Echinopsis peruviana), and as well in a number of other members of the Cactaceae plant family. It is also found in small amounts in certain members of the Fabaceae (bean) family, including Acacia berlandieri.
Molecular biology	Molecular biology is the branch of biology that deals with the molecular basis of biological activity. This field overlaps with other areas of biology and chemistry, particularly genetics and biochemistry. Molecular biology chiefly concerns itself with understanding the interactions between the various systems of a cell, including the interactions between the different types of DNA, RNA and protein biosynthesis as well as learning how these interactions are regulated.
Molecular evolution	Molecular evolution is a change in the sequence composition of cellular molecules such as DNA, RNA, and proteins over long periods of time. Molecular evolution attempts to explain biological change at the molecular and cellular level using the principles of evolutionary biology and population genetics. Major topics in molecular evolution concern the rates and impacts of single nucleotide change, neutral evolution vs. natural selection, origins of new genes, the genetic nature of complex traits, the genetic basis of speciation, evolution of development, and ways that evolutionary forces influence genomic and phenotypic changes.
Tetrodotoxin	Tetrodotoxin, frequently abbreviated as TTX, is a potent neurotoxin with no known receptor antagonist. There have been successful tests of a possible neurochemical in mice, but further tests must be carried out to determine efficacy in humans. Fampridine has been shown to reverse tetrodotoxin toxicity in animal experiments.

1. In the field of biochemistry, a _____ is a molecule usually found on the surface of a cell, that receives chemical signals from outside the cell. When such external substances bind to a _____, they direct the cell to do something, such as divide, die, or allow specific substances to enter or exit the cell.

   _____s are proteins embedded in either the cell's plasma membrane (cell surface _____s), in the cytoplasm, or in the cell's nucleus (nuclear _____s), to which specific signaling molecules may attach.

   a. Bacterial outer membrane
   b. Biofilm
   c. Biological membrane
   d. Receptor

2. _____s are endogenous chemicals that transmit signals from a neuron to a target cell across a synapse. _____s are packaged into synaptic vesicles clustered beneath the membrane in the axon terminal, on the presynaptic side of a synapse. They are released into and diffuse across the synaptic cleft, where they bind to specific receptors in the membrane on the postsynaptic side of the synapse.

   a. 3-Hydroxyaspartic acid
   b. Chaconine
   c. Glycoalkaloid
   d. Neurotransmitter

3. In a sensory system, a _____ is a sensory nerve ending that responds to a stimulus in the internal or external environment of an organism. In response to stimuli, the _____ initiates sensory transduction by creating graded potentials or action potentials in the same cell or in an adjacent one.

   a. Baroreceptor
   b. Bulboid corpuscle
   c. Campaniform sensilla
   d. Sensory receptor

4. _____ is a change in the sequence composition of cellular molecules such as DNA, RNA, and proteins over long periods of time. _____ attempts to explain biological change at the molecular and cellular level using the principles of evolutionary biology and population genetics. Major topics in _____ concern the rates and impacts of single nucleotide change, neutral evolution vs. natural selection, origins of new genes, the genetic nature of complex traits, the genetic basis of speciation, evolution of development, and ways that evolutionary forces influence genomic and phenotypic changes.

   a. 3-Hydroxyaspartic acid
   b. Chaconine
   c. Molecular evolution
   d. Solamargine

5. In biochemistry, an _____ molecule is usually a small molecule that selectively binds to a protein and regulates its biological activity. In this manner, _____ molecules act as ligands that can increase or decrease enzyme activity, gene expression, or cell signalling. _____ molecules can also directly regulate the activity of some mRNA molecules (riboswitches).

   a. 14-3-3 protein
   b. Bacterioferritin
   c. Effector
   d. Bcl-2-associated death promoter

ANSWER KEY
21. Nervous Systems

1. d
2. d
3. d
4. c
5. c

You can take the complete Chapter Practice Test

for 21. Nervous Systems
on all key terms, persons, places, and concepts.

Online 99 Cents

http://www.JustTheFacts101.com

Use www.JustTheFacts101.com for all your study needs

including Facts101's online interactive problem solving labs in

chemistry, statistics, mathematics, and more.

CHAPTER OUTLINE: KEY TERMS, PEOPLE, PLACES, CONCEPTS

	Molecular genetics
	Pheromone

CHAPTER HIGHLIGHTS & NOTES: KEY TERMS, PEOPLE, PLACES, CONCEPTS

Molecular genetics	Molecular genetics is the field of biology and genetics that studies the structure and function of genes at a molecular level. Molecular genetics employs the methods of genetics and molecular biology to elucidate molecular function and interactions among genes. It is so called to differentiate it from other sub fields of genetics such as ecological genetics and population genetics.
Pheromone	A pheromone is a secreted or excreted chemical factor that triggers a social response in members of the same species. Pheromones are chemicals capable of acting outside the body of the secreting individual to impact the behavior of the receiving individual. There are alarm pheromones, food trail pheromones, sex pheromones, and many others that affect behavior or physiology.

CHAPTER QUIZ: KEY TERMS, PEOPLE, PLACES, CONCEPTS

1. A _____ is a secreted or excreted chemical factor that triggers a social response in members of the same species. _____s are chemicals capable of acting outside the body of the secreting individual to impact the behavior of the receiving individual. There are alarm _____s, food trail _____s, sex _____s, and many others that affect behavior or physiology.

   a. 3-Hydroxyaspartic acid
   b. Chaconine
   c. Pheromone
   d. Solamargine

2. . _____ is the field of biology and genetics that studies the structure and function of genes at a molecular level. _____ employs the methods of genetics and molecular biology to elucidate molecular function and interactions among genes. It is so called to differentiate it from other sub fields of genetics such as ecological genetics and population genetics.

   a. Bacterial artificial chromosome

b. Molecular genetics

c. BamHI

d. Base calling

1. c
2. b

You can take the complete Chapter Practice Test

for 22. Behavior
on all key terms, persons, places, and concepts.

Online 99 Cents

http://www.JustTheFacts101.com

Use www.JustTheFacts101.com for all your study needs

including Facts101's online interactive problem solving labs in

chemistry, statistics, mathematics, and more.

23. Immune Systems

CHAPTER OUTLINE: KEY TERMS, PEOPLE, PLACES, CONCEPTS

	Antigen
	Cowpox
	Polio vaccine
	Cytokine
	Protein
	Antibody
	Complement system
	Histamine

CHAPTER HIGHLIGHTS & NOTES: KEY TERMS, PEOPLE, PLACES, CONCEPTS

Antigen

In immunology, an antigen is the substance that binds specifically to the respective antibody. Each antibody from the diverse repertoire binds a specific antigenic structure by means of its variable region interaction (CDR loops), an analogy is the fit between a lock and a key. Paul Ehrlich coined the term antibody (in German Antikörper) in his side-chain theory at the end of 19th century.

Cowpox

Cowpox is a skin disease caused by a virus known as the cowpox virus. The pox is related to the vaccinia virus and got its name from the distribution of the disease when dairymaids touched the udders of infected cows. The ailment manifests itself in the form of red blisters, and is transmitted by touch from infected animals to humans.

Polio vaccine

Two polio vaccines are used throughout the world to combat poliomyelitis . The first was developed by Jonas Salk and first tested in 1952. Announced to the world by Dr Thomas Francis Junior on April 12 1955, it consists of an injected dose of inactivated (dead) poliovirus. An oral vaccine was developed by Albert Sabin using attenuated poliovirus.

Cytokine

Cytokines are a diverse group of soluble proteins, peptides, or glycoproteins which act as hormonal regulators or signaling molecules at nano- to- picomolar concentrations and help in cell signaling. The term 'cytokine' encompasses a large and diverse family of regulators produced throughout the body by cells of diverse embryological origin.

23. Immune Systems

CHAPTER HIGHLIGHTS & NOTES: KEY TERMS, PEOPLE, PLACES, CONCEPTS

Protein	Proteins are large biological molecules, or macromolecules, consisting of one or more chains of amino acids. Proteins perform a vast array of functions within living organisms, including catalyzing metabolic reactions, replicating DNA, responding to stimuli, and transporting molecules from one location to another. Proteins differ from one another primarily in their sequence of amino acids, which is dictated by the nucleotide sequence of their genes, and which usually results in folding of the protein into a specific three-dimensional structure that determines its activity.
Antibody	An antibody, also known as an immunoglobulin (Ig), is a large Y-shaped protein produced by B cells that is used by the immune system to identify and neutralize foreign objects such as bacteria and viruses. The antibody recognizes a unique part of the foreign target, called an antigen. Each tip of the 'Y' of an antibody contains a paratope (a structure analogous to a lock) that is specific for one particular epitope (similarly analogous to a key) on an antigen, allowing these two structures to bind together with precision.
Complement system	The complement system helps or "complements" the ability of antibodies and phagocytic cells to clear pathogens from an organism. It is part of the immune system called the innate immune system that is not adaptable and does not change over the course of an individual's lifetime. However, it can be recruited and brought into action by the adaptive immune system.
Histamine	Histamine is an organic nitrogen compound involved in local immune responses as well as regulating physiological function in the gut and acting as a neurotransmitter. Histamine triggers the inflammatory response. As part of an immune response to foreign pathogens, histamine is produced by basophils and by mast cells found in nearby connective tissues.

CHAPTER QUIZ: KEY TERMS, PEOPLE, PLACES, CONCEPTS

1. The _____ helps or "complements" the ability of antibodies and phagocytic cells to clear pathogens from an organism. It is part of the immune system called the innate immune system that is not adaptable and does not change over the course of an individual's lifetime. However, it can be recruited and brought into action by the adaptive immune system.

   a. Cystic fibrosis transmembrane conductance regulator
   b. Sterolin
   c. TAP1
   d. Complement system

2. . An _____, also known as an immunoglobulin (Ig), is a large Y-shaped protein produced by B cells that is used by the immune system to identify and neutralize foreign objects such as bacteria and viruses. The _____ recognizes a unique part of the foreign target, called an antigen.

Visit Cram101.com for full Practice Exams

Each tip of the 'Y' of an _____ contains a paratope (a structure analogous to a lock) that is specific for one particular epitope (similarly analogous to a key) on an antigen, allowing these two structures to bind together with precision.

a. 3-Hydroxyaspartic acid
b. Chaconine
c. Antibody
d. Solamargine

3. _____ is an organic nitrogen compound involved in local immune responses as well as regulating physiological function in the gut and acting as a neurotransmitter. _____ triggers the inflammatory response. As part of an immune response to foreign pathogens, _____ is produced by basophils and by mast cells found in nearby connective tissues.

a. Histamine
b. Dimaprit
c. N-Acetylserotonin
d. 3-Hydroxyaspartic acid

4. In immunology, an _____ is the substance that binds specifically to the respective antibody. Each antibody from the diverse repertoire binds a specific antigenic structure by means of its variable region interaction (CDR loops), an analogy is the fit between a lock and a key. Paul Ehrlich coined the term antibody (in German Antikörper) in his side-chain theory at the end of 19th century.

a. 6-Monoacetylmorphine
b. Biomolecule
c. DARPin
d. Antigen

5. Two _____s are used throughout the world to combat poliomyelitis . The first was developed by Jonas Salk and first tested in 1952. Announced to the world by Dr Thomas Francis Junior on April 12 1955, it consists of an injected dose of inactivated (dead) poliovirus. An oral vaccine was developed by Albert Sabin using attenuated poliovirus.

a. British Polio Fellowship
b. Charles Armstrong
c. Polio vaccine
d. David Bodian

1. d
2. c
3. a
4. d
5. c

You can take the complete Chapter Practice Test

for 23. Immune Systems
on all key terms, persons, places, and concepts.

Online 99 Cents

http://www.JustTheFacts101.com

Use www.JustTheFacts101.com for all your study needs

including Facts101's online interactive problem solving labs in

chemistry, statistics, mathematics, and more.

24. Ecosystem Structure and Function

Nutrient

DNA sequencing

Nutrient

A nutrient is a chemical that an organism needs to live and grow or a substance used in an organism's metabolism which must be taken in from its environment. They are used to build and repair tissues, regulate body processes and are converted to and used as energy. Methods for nutrient intake vary, with animals and protists consuming foods that are digested by an internal digestive system, but most plants ingest nutrients directly from the soil through their roots or from the atmosphere.

DNA sequencing

DNA sequencing is the process of determining the precise order of nucleotides within a DNA molecule. It includes any method or technology that is used to determine the order of the four bases--adenine, guanine, cytosine, and thymine--in a strand of DNA. The advent of rapid DNA sequencing methods has greatly accelerated biological and medical research and discovery.

Knowledge of DNA sequences has become indispensable for basic biological research, and in numerous applied fields such as diagnostic, biotechnology, forensic biology, and biological systematics.

1. A _____ is a chemical that an organism needs to live and grow or a substance used in an organism's metabolism which must be taken in from its environment. They are used to build and repair tissues, regulate body processes and are converted to and used as energy. Methods for _____ intake vary, with animals and protists consuming foods that are digested by an internal digestive system, but most plants ingest _____s directly from the soil through their roots or from the atmosphere.

   a. 3-Hydroxyaspartic acid
   b. Chaconine
   c. Glycoalkaloid
   d. Nutrient

2. _____ is the process of determining the precise order of nucleotides within a DNA molecule. It includes any method or technology that is used to determine the order of the four bases--adenine, guanine, cytosine, and thymine-- in a strand of DNA. The advent of rapid _____ methods has greatly accelerated biological and medical research and discovery.

   Knowledge of DNA sequences has become indispensable for basic biological research, and in numerous applied fields such as diagnostic, biotechnology, forensic biology, and biological systematics.

   a. Bacterial artificial chromosome
   b. Bacterial conjugation
   c. BamHI
   d. DNA sequencing

1. d

2. d

You can take the complete Chapter Practice Test

for 24. Ecosystem Structure and Function
on all key terms, persons, places, and concepts.

Online 99 Cents

http://www.JustTheFacts101.com

Use www.JustTheFacts101.com for all your study needs

including Facts101's online interactive problem solving labs in

chemistry, statistics, mathematics, and more.

25. Change in Ecosystems

CHAPTER OUTLINE: KEY TERMS, PEOPLE, PLACES, CONCEPTS

Kudzu

Growth hormone

Hormone

Nitric oxide

Amylase

Cell division

Genetic code

Transcription

Transfer RNA

DNA repair

Molecular genetics

Frequency

Molecular evolution

Sensory receptor

Receptor

Human genome

Antibody

Kudzu	Kudzu, also called Japanese arrowroot, is a plant in the pea family Fabaceae, subfamily Faboideae. It is a climbing, coiling, and trailing vine native to much of eastern Asia, southeast Asia, and some Pacific Islands. Its name comes from the Japanese name for the plant, kuzu , which was written 'kudzu' in historical romanizations.
Growth hormone	Growth hormone, also known as somatotropin or somatropin, is a peptide hormone that stimulates growth, cell reproduction and regeneration in humans and other animals. It is a type of mitogen which is specific only to certain kinds of cells. Growth hormone is a 191-amino acid, single-chain polypeptide that is synthesized, stored, and secreted by somatotropic cells within the lateral wings of the anterior pituitary gland.
Hormone	A hormone is a chemical released by a cell, a gland, or an organ in one part of the body that affects cells in other parts of the organism. Generally, only a small amount of hormone is required to alter cell metabolism. In essence, it is a chemical messenger that transports a signal from one cell to another.
Nitric oxide	Nitric oxide, or nitrogen oxide, also known as nitrogen monoxide, is a molecule with chemical formula NO. It is a free radical and is an important intermediate in the chemical industry. Nitric oxide is a by-product of combustion of substances in the air, as in automobile engines, fossil fuel power plants, and is produced naturally during the electrical discharges of lightning in thunderstorms. In mammals including humans, NO is an important cellular signaling molecule involved in many physiological and pathological processes.
Amylase	Amylase is an enzyme that catalyses the hydrolysis of starch into sugars. Amylase is present in the saliva of humans and some other mammals, where it begins the chemical process of digestion. Foods that contain much starch but little sugar, such as rice and potato, taste slightly sweet as they are chewed because amylase turns some of their starch into sugar in the mouth.
Cell division	Cell division is the process by which a parent cell divides into two or more daughter cells. Cell division usually occurs as part of a larger cell cycle. In eukaryotes, there are two distinct type of cell division: a vegetative division, whereby each daughter cell is genetically identical to the parent cell (mitosis), and a reductive cell division, whereby the number of chromosomes in the daughter cells is reduced by half, to produce haploid gametes (meiosis).
Genetic code	The genetic code is the set of rules by which information encoded within genetic material is translated into proteins by living cells. Biological decoding is accomplished by the ribosome, which links amino acids in an order specified by mRNA, using transfer RNA (tRNA) molecules to carry amino acids and to read the mRNA three nucleotides at a time. The genetic code is highly similar among all organisms and can be expressed in a simple table with 64 entries.

25. Change in Ecosystems

Transcription	Transcription is the first step of gene expression, in which a particular segment of DNA is copied into RNA by the enzyme, RNA polymerase. Both RNA and DNA are nucleic acids, which use base pairs of nucleotides as a complementary language that can be converted back and forth from DNA to RNA by the action of the correct enzymes. During transcription, a DNA sequence is read by an RNA polymerase, which produces a complementary, antiparallel RNA strand.
Transfer RNA	A Transfer RNA is an adaptor molecule composed of RNA, typically 73 to 94 nucleotides in length, that serves as the physical link between the nucleotide sequence of nucleic acids (DNA and RNA) and the amino acid sequence of proteins. It does this by carrying an amino acid to the protein synthetic machinery of a cell (ribosome) as directed by a three-nucleotide sequence (codon) in a messenger RNA (mRNA). As such, tRNAs are a necessary component of protein translation, the biological synthesis of new proteins according to the genetic code.
DNA repair	DNA repair is a collection of processes by which a cell identifies and corrects damage to the DNA molecules that encode its genome. In human cells, both normal metabolic activities and environmental factors such as UV light and radiation can cause DNA damage, resulting in as many as 1 million individual molecular lesions per cell per day. Many of these lesions cause structural damage to the DNA molecule and can alter or eliminate the cell's ability to transcribe the gene that the affected DNA encodes.
Molecular genetics	Molecular genetics is the field of biology and genetics that studies the structure and function of genes at a molecular level. Molecular genetics employs the methods of genetics and molecular biology to elucidate molecular function and interactions among genes. It is so called to differentiate it from other sub fields of genetics such as ecological genetics and population genetics.
Frequency	Frequency is a gene discovered in the fungus Neurospora crassa in 1978 that encodes the protein frequency. The gene is 2,980bp long in Sordaria macrospora k-hell. The FRQ protein plays a key role in the autoregulatory transcription translation negative feedback loop (TTFL), which is responsible for circadian rhythms in N. crassa and other fungi such as N. sitophita, N. tetrasperma, N. galapagosensis, C. spinulosa, and L. australiensis.
Molecular evolution	Molecular evolution is a change in the sequence composition of cellular molecules such as DNA, RNA, and proteins over long periods of time. Molecular evolution attempts to explain biological change at the molecular and cellular level using the principles of evolutionary biology and population genetics. Major topics in molecular evolution concern the rates and impacts of single nucleotide change, neutral evolution vs. natural selection, origins of new genes, the genetic nature of complex traits, the genetic basis of speciation, evolution of development, and ways that evolutionary forces influence genomic and phenotypic changes.
Sensory receptor	In a sensory system, a sensory receptor is a sensory nerve ending that responds to a stimulus in the internal or external environment of an organism.

In response to stimuli, the sensory receptor initiates sensory transduction by creating graded potentials or action potentials in the same cell or in an adjacent one.

Receptor	In the field of biochemistry, a receptor is a molecule usually found on the surface of a cell, that receives chemical signals from outside the cell. When such external substances bind to a receptor, they direct the cell to do something, such as divide, die, or allow specific substances to enter or exit the cell.
	Receptors are proteins embedded in either the cell's plasma membrane (cell surface receptors), in the cytoplasm, or in the cell's nucleus (nuclear receptors), to which specific signaling molecules may attach.
Human genome	The human genome is the complete set of genetic information for humans . This information is located as DNA sequences within the 23 chromosome pairs in cell nuclei and in a small DNA molecule found within individual mitochondria. Human genomes include both protein-coding DNA genes and noncoding DNA. Haploid human genomes (contained in egg and sperm cells) consist of three billion DNA base pairs, while diploid genomes (found in somatic cells) have twice the DNA content.
Antibody	An antibody, also known as an immunoglobulin (Ig), is a large Y-shaped protein produced by B cells that is used by the immune system to identify and neutralize foreign objects such as bacteria and viruses. The antibody recognizes a unique part of the foreign target, called an antigen. Each tip of the 'Y' of an antibody contains a paratope (a structure analogous to a lock) that is specific for one particular epitope (similarly analogous to a key) on an antigen, allowing these two structures to bind together with precision.

CHAPTER QUIZ: KEY TERMS, PEOPLE, PLACES, CONCEPTS

1. _____ is a collection of processes by which a cell identifies and corrects damage to the DNA molecules that encode its genome. In human cells, both normal metabolic activities and environmental factors such as UV light and radiation can cause DNA damage, resulting in as many as 1 million individual molecular lesions per cell per day. Many of these lesions cause structural damage to the DNA molecule and can alter or eliminate the cell's ability to transcribe the gene that the affected DNA encodes.

   a. DNA repair
   b. Chaconine
   c. Glycoalkaloid
   d. Solamargine

2. . _____, also called Japanese arrowroot, is a plant in the pea family Fabaceae, subfamily Faboideae. It is a climbing, coiling, and trailing vine native to much of eastern Asia, southeast Asia, and some Pacific Islands. Its name comes from the Japanese name for the plant, kuzu , which was written '_____' in historical romanizations.

a. Corn starch

b. Corn syrup

c. Dextrose equivalent

d. Kudzu

3. In the field of biochemistry, a _____ is a molecule usually found on the surface of a cell, that receives chemical signals from outside the cell. When such external substances bind to a _____, they direct the cell to do something, such as divide, die, or allow specific substances to enter or exit the cell.

_____s are proteins embedded in either the cell's plasma membrane (cell surface _____s), in the cytoplasm, or in the cell's nucleus (nuclear _____s), to which specific signaling molecules may attach.

a. Bacterial outer membrane

b. Biofilm

c. Biological membrane

d. Receptor

4. _____ is the field of biology and genetics that studies the structure and function of genes at a molecular level. _____ employs the methods of genetics and molecular biology to elucidate molecular function and interactions among genes. It is so called to differentiate it from other sub fields of genetics such as ecological genetics and population genetics.

a. Bacterial artificial chromosome

b. Bacterial conjugation

c. BamHI

d. Molecular genetics

5. The _____ is the complete set of genetic information for humans . This information is located as DNA sequences within the 23 chromosome pairs in cell nuclei and in a small DNA molecule found within individual mitochondria. _____s include both protein-coding DNA genes and noncoding DNA. Haploid _____s (contained in egg and sperm cells) consist of three billion DNA base pairs, while diploid genomes (found in somatic cells) have twice the DNA content.

a. Human genome

b. Bifidobacterium longum

c. Bombyx mori

d. Botryllus schlosseri

1. a
2. d
3. d
4. d
5. a

You can take the complete Chapter Practice Test

for 25. Change in Ecosystems
on all key terms, persons, places, and concepts.

Online 99 Cents

http://www.JustTheFacts101.com

Use www.JustTheFacts101.com for all your study needs

including Facts101's online interactive problem solving labs in

chemistry, statistics, mathematics, and more.

Want More?
JustTheFacts101.com...

**Jtf101.com provides the outlines and highlights of
your textbooks, just like this e-StudyGuide, but also
gives you the PRACTICE TESTS, and other exclusive
study tools for all of your textbooks.**

Learn More. *Just click*
http://www.JustTheFacts101.com/

CPSIA information can be obtained at www.ICGtesting.com
Printed in the USA
BVOW06s1733291114

376863BV00002B/13/P